SOCIAL NETWORKS AND MARITAL INTERACTION

By Charles E. Grantham

PALO ALTO, CALIFORNIA

Published By

R & E Research Associates, Inc.

936 Industrial Avenue
Palo Alto, California 94303

PUBLISHERS

Library of Congress Card Catalog Number

81-83621

I.S.B.N.

0-88247-617-3

HQ
536
. 67
1981

To Ellen, Jean and Gregory

ACKNOWLEDGEMENTS

I wish to thank the members of my dissertation committee for their encouragement, advice and patience. Foremost among them was Professor Robert W. Janes and Dr. Sam Silbergeld. Dr. Barbara Meeker provided expert guidance in methodological matters and sound practical advice. Professor Edward Dager's insightful comments also made the final work useful to both clinicians and those more academically oriented. Dr. Steven Rosen brought much to the work through his perspective as an anthropologist.

I also wish to acknowledge the access given to me by the National Institute of Mental Health, Mental Health Study Center. Needless to say, the research reported here, would have been impossible without access to the unique data set which was provided. NIMH's sponsorship of the project and myself while the study was being completed were invaluable.

Finally a debt of gratitude goes to Mrs. Dorothy Simmons, Karen Sheehan and Terry Bowers for the countless hours of typing, editing, retyping and checking every last detail.

PREFACE

This monograph was inspired by the powerful ideas of Gregory Bateson. It was the inspiration of his thinking that gave birth to the research which was conducted. Of course, the practical requirement of completing a dissertation provided additional motivation to complete the study and disseminate the results.

What follows is a revised version of the initial manuscript. I have endeavored, whereever possible, to provide additional information based on the critical comments provided by several anonymous reviewers, colleagues and friends who have read portions of the manuscript. Any error in interpretation of data and associated conclusions remains my sole responsibilty.

Readers of this book should take it for exactly what it is: a report of an initial exploration into a new realm of social network research. The data are unique, the methodology newly derived and the conclusions subject to modification based on additional research. This work is not the alpha omega of network research. It began as an attempt to verify some underlying assumptions of classical work in the field and ended pursuing uncharted pathways for future research.

The major contribution this monograph presents is the sensitization of researchers to the utility of employing new theories, i.e., Bateson and Kemper, and exploratory analytic methodologies to existing lines of research. If this book does nothing more than help network researchers take a step back and look at their data from a slightly different perspective, it will have accomplished its purpose.

TABLE OF CONTENTS

X

LIST OF TABLES

XI

LIST OF FIGURES

FIGURE

XIII

CHAPTER 1

INTRODUCTION

A practical problem in social psychiatry constitutes the impetus for this study. The management of anxiety and hostility, an important clinical issue for psychiatry, may be accomplished through intervention in informal social structures such as social networks (Henderson, 1980). The application of sociological theory and methodology to this issue, permits an inductive orientation to be coupled to unique solutions (Hyman, 1967:121). The study reported here is an example of sociology applied to an examination of the relationship between the individual and the social environment within the context of mental health (Myers, 1965:332).

The prototypical model for this investigation is found in Bott's Family and Social Network (1957) in which Lewin's (1935) field theory is used as a basic conceptual framework. It this framework, most behavior is seen as a function of a person in a social situation, and performance of roles is viewed as a function of needs and preferences in relation to tasks, the immediate social environment, and recognized norm of behavior. Social networks are seen as informal social structures that mediate between individual and society.

Bott (1957:60) states that the provision of emotional support in social networks of spouses lessens the supportive demands made by spouses in their dyadic relationship. However, Bott did not examine the relative influence of structural characteristics of individual spouse networks and connections between these networks upon specific psychological affects associated with interaction between spouses. Bott (1957) assumed that an inverse relationship existed

1

between amount of emotional communication (in networks) and anxiety and hostility found during marital interaction. Fischer (1977:36) identifies several factors which are related to the amount of emotional communication in social networks, they are: network size, density, amount of effective communication between a person and each network member, and source of network membership. In addition, connection between spouse networks may effect this basic relationship between communication and psychological affects. Weiss (1967:43) states that a range of relational functions must be performed in each spouse social network in order to prevent the generation of anxiety and hostility in the marital relationship. Therefore, this problem may be translated into general research question:

(1) Is there an inverse relationship between social network size, density, type and frequency of communication, inter-connection with other social networks, source of network membership and anxiety/hostility levels associated with marital interaction?

(2) Are there different patterns of emotional communication (i.e., method, frequency) in different areas of social networks defined on a basis of source of network membership?

The structure and function of social networks are important considerations in the analysis of human behavior.

People are members of multiple social networks and the structure of these multiple networks may not be coterminous. A person's relationship to the formal organizational structure of society is multi-faceted and is separated into several categories of role relations (Frankenberg, 1969). Weiss (1969), in his analysis of the function social networks have for the individual, echoes the point that multiple network structures provide a differentiated mechanism by which society may shape a person's thinking and acting. A person received his or her understanding of social reality, moral values, goal, and sense of self from these social networks.

In terms of structure and function, an analysis of a person's social network allows for an examination of

2

he interactional properties of informal social tructure. The research reported below assumes that >cial networks, as informal social structures, provide n individual with consensual definitions and iterpretations of behavior. Within the context of an dult's multiple social networks, the marital elationship serves the function of intimacy. The tructure of a person's social network, outside this itimate context, may be expected to impact upon and ifluence the patterns of behavior found in the marital elationship. The structure and function of social etworks are closely related, and behavior in one >rtion of a network may be influenced by the structure r function of another area (Weiss, 1969, 1974). (See igure 1)

The present research examines the relationship etween (a) the manner in which a person is linked to he community social structure, and (b) the iaracteristics of a person's relationship to their >ouse. The manner in which a person is located within ie community structure, or larger social organization, ay be determined from an examination of the attributes f that person's social network. A person's elationship to their spouse may be characterized by ie psychological affects associated with interaction etween spouses. While this goal follows from Bott's .957) work, it may be seen as a further elaboration of er work in that social network measures will be pecifically defined based on an examination of the ifferentiated structure and function of social etworks.

Most investigations in using the concept of social etwork implicitly follow Bott's (1957) assumption that n inverse relationship exists between the provision of >cial support and the presence of negative affect. ecent reviews of the literature (Mueller, 1980) and ieoretical formulations (Pattison, 1975) indicate this elationship to be much more complete than originally hought. Furthermore, the emerging sociological >proach to emotional life (Kemper, 1978; Shott, 1980) rovides additional and relevant insight into the >mplicated process by which social structures may ifluence emotions experienced by social actors. Thus, iough this research constitutes an empirical effort to alidate Bott's (1957) assumption, it also will icorporate current perspectives.

For example, this research incorporates the use of >mplex indicators of discrete emotional states which have not been used previously in relation to social networks. it also utilizes a demographically homogeneous sample, that results in control of indicator covariation which may otherwise be attributed to social class.

The scope of this endeavor extends only to an examination of the relationship among self-reported behavioral measures of the social networks of husband and wife as well as specific affects associated with interaction between spouses. Measurement of subject attitudes toward network members and determination of the exact nature of the communicational exchanges among network members lies beyond the present scope. Findings will apply to their appropriate, but necessarily restricted context.

Figure 1

"Network Relational Function, Source, and Associated Affects"1

Network Relational Function	Structural Source Within Network	Affective Results Expected due to Deficiency
Intimacy	Spouse, Marriage	Loneliness
Social Integration	Friends, Colleagues	Isolation, Boredom
Opportunity for Nurturant Behavior	Family, Parents	Meaningless
Reassurance of Personal Worth	Friends, Colleagues	Loss of Self-esteem
Assistance (Information, Service)	Family, Kinship	Vulnerability, Anxiety

4

[1]Adapted from Weiss, Robert S., "The Fund of Sociability," <u>Transaction</u> 6, 1969, p. 36-43.

CHAPTER 2

THEORETICAL PERSPECTIVE

AND REVIEW OF SELECTED LITERATURE

The following discussion begins with a definitio of key terms and a general outline of the importance history, and use of social networks as a concept i social research. Following this, a specific discussio of the structure and function of social networks wil link the current literature and theoretica explanations to the dynamics of relationships amon study variables. In conclusion, research hypothese will be stated in terms that provide a basis of linkin analytic results to current theoretical understanding of social networks and their effect on socia interaction.

Definition of Key Terms

Before beginning an exegesis of social networ theory it is useful to clarify the central conceptua issues which surround the topic in the literature. On conceptual problem, concerning the analytic use o social networks in empirical research, is th differentiation of structural and processua descriptions of networks. Structure may be considere as process over time (Buckley, 1968:20-21). Given th context of this research, i.e., cross-sectional i nature, structural and processual measures of network are analytically indistinguishable. Stated anothe way, structural characteristics of networks, such a density and size, are viewed as being of the sam logical order as process characteristics of networks such as frequency of communication (Bateson, 1979:84

85).

In the discussion below it is shown that each researcher who has used the concept of social network in their studies has chosen to operationally define social network, social support network, structure of network, and function of network in a slightly different way. This lack of consensual definition and specification of the relationship between structure and function hinders the development of a uniform approach to network analysis. Therefore, it is necessary to specify meanings of key terms for the present study prior to a theoretical discussion.

Social support networks are seen as a subset of social relations within the larger social network of a person for the purpose of this research. (See Figure 2.) The characteristic which differentiates a social support network is emotional communication; social networks possess "social support" to various degrees. Communications within a social support network is primarily emotional in nature; whereas the communication within a social network, outside of the social support network is primarily instrumental in nature. Although it is recognized that there is some overlap between these two patterns of communication, the overlap will be assumed to be negligible here to facilitate analysis.

Many authors have defined, and analyzed, social networks in terms of their structure (Frankenberg, 1968) while other have conducted the same type of analysis using functional definitions (Cobb, 1976; Warren, 1976). Still other researchers have combined both structural and functional descriptions in their analysis of social networks (Weiss, 1979). This variance in social network definition and measurement has led to a lack of study comparability in the literature. Again, for the purpose of this research the structure of a social network, and its lesser included concept, social support network, will be defined in terms of patterns of communication such as method, type, kind, frequency, and number of communication linkages.

The functions served by social networks are many and varied. The research reported here is focused on only one of these functions: social support. However, social support may be viewed as composed of many finer functional distinctions such as ego enhancement, value validation etc. (Warren, 1976). In summary, the literature reveals a wide range of conceptual

7

Figure 2

"Diagram of Relationship Between Social Networks, Social Support Networks and Types of Communication"

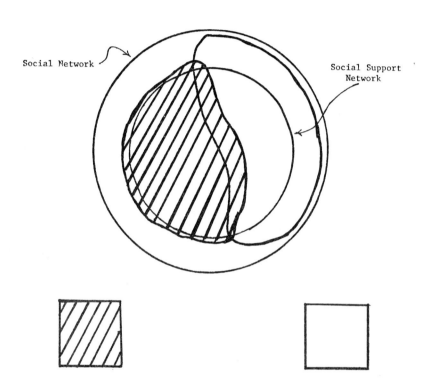

Area of Emotional
Communication

Area of Instrumental
Communication

approaches and operational definitions of social networks. It is not the purpose here to offer a unifying perspective on social support networks, but merely to investigate the relationship of network structure, in a very specific sense, to one function social networks serve for the individual.

Theoretical Background of Research Question

The central question which this research addresses is: How does participation in specific group interaction effect the individual? Aside from the applied genesis of this study, this question has been historically central to sociology. Durkheim's (1897) classical study of suicide implicitly attempted to answer this same question by correlating measures of social integration with individual acts of deviant behavior. Perhaps, the most cogent theoretical basis for the sociological analysis of social networks is found in the works of Georg Simmel (1908). A brief review of the ideas expressed by these sociologists will serve to illustrate the point that social networks and their effect upon individuals has been central to sociology.

Durkheim (1897) hypothesized that individuals commit "egotistical" suicide when they lacked social bonding to others. Curiously, Durkheim's work illustrated the point that social networks, or social integration in his terms, could both control acts of deviant behavior and also be seen as a casual factor related to such behavior. Social bonding brought about consensual definitions of appropriate behavior and acted as a social control force, thus preventing the occurrence of many deviant acts. If egotistical suicide is viewed as the supreme act of hostility toward self, then Durkheim's analysis indicates that a lack of group interaction, through the form of social networks, could be casually related to the generation of hostility directed inward. Durkheim's work, like this study, was concerned with the question of how group interaction effects the individual.

Georg Simmel's critical influence on American sociology is well documented as being related to the development of the discipline in the United States (Levine, Carter, and Gorman, 1976). Much of Simmel's work concerned itself with the analysis of sociological forms or more appropriately, forms of social structure

9

(Simmel, 1902, 1908). Particularly important, for the purposes of this discussion, was Simmel's interest in how the number of people in a group effected another person's behavior (Simmel, 1902). Simmel's analysis demonstrated that changing the number of social interactants from two to three has a profound effect upon the relationships of all group members (Simmel, in Wolff, 1950). Simmel felt that the number of group members was a critical factor in determining, shaping, and controlling human behavior. Again, it appears that analysis of social networks as a method of connecting a person to the larger social group has been a central focus of sociology.

The explicit study of social networks is a nascent perspective of sociology (Leinhardt, 1977). Following from the work of Durkheim and Simmel, social network, as an analytical concept, has been employed in social research which attempts to elaborate the linkages between social structure and individual behavior. The work of the symbolic interactionists (Mead, 1934) incorporate the concept of social network in their theoretical discussions. The idea that the concept of self develops only through interaction with others is an implicit recognition of the effect group interaction has upon the individual at a psychological level. All of these approaches, theories and classical works have lain the groundwork for the recent emergence of social networks as an explicit focus of sociological research.

The emphasis on the importance of social networks in shaping behavior has also been linked to the work of social anthropologist (Barnes, 1954; Frankenberg, 1969; and Boissevain, 1974). Barnes (1954) used the network perspective to examine the association of class and community membership in small, rural Norwegian communities. Barnes's basic finding was that the structure of social networks appeared to vary by class position. Frankenberg (1969) used the concept of social network to develop a theory of social change in British rural communities during the process of urbanization. Frankenberg's theory describes social change in terms of changing social network structure, where rural social networks are found to be more dense and less extensive than those found in urban communities. Boissevain (1974) investigated social networks structure to describe systems of reciprocal instrumental exchange among friends reporting that consensual values of reciprocity were the values, and consequence norms, that held social networks together

10

ving them structural stability.

The studies reported above have been primarily
ocused at investigating social networks within the
ontext of non-clinical, normal populations. The
enesis of this study, however, requires a finer focus
n the role social networks may play in the generation
f mental disorder. In discussing the theoretical
mportance of investigating social networks, and the
esser included concept, social support networks,
nderson (1977:185-191) states:

> Solid bonds are proposed as essential for
> obtaining a commodity commonly but
> unsatisfactorily referred to as support...it
> is apparent that individuals have, quite
> simply, a requirement for affectively
> positive interaction with others. When
> support is lacking, there is evidence that
> psychiatric and perhaps medical morbidity
> rates increase.

ther investigators (e.g., Cassel,1976; Kessler, 1979;
nd Liem and Liem, 1978), report evidence which
uggests that social support networks may intervene
etween social structure and the individual.

Recently, the concept of social network has become
he central feature of research on the relationship of
he social environment to psychiatric disorder.
eller (1980), in his review of the relationship
etween social networks and the etiology and
tenuation of psychiatric disorder, finds that the
tructure, function, and dynamics of social networks
ay influence the onset and course of affective
isorders such as depression. Pattison (1977:217)
ates, "For some years there has been growing
recognition that emotional disorder, in part, has its
oots in the social milieu of the individual." In
ummary, then, there exists suggestive evidence that
ocial networks may play a rose, in generation and
revention of mental disorder. Further, the work of
ttison (1977) and Mueller (1980) has lain the
oundation for empirical research into the relationship
etween social networks and mental disorders.

Social Network Structure

A central problem in network analysis is the

11

identification of indicators of network structure which may be associated with measures of the social process under investigation. In other words, what are the parameters of network structure which may be empirically associated with specific patterns of interpersonal communication? Investigators working in the tradition of social anthropology, Barnes (1954) and Mitchell (1969), have made attempts to identify parameters of the social interaction process using social network as a key analytical variable. One of the first systematic attempts at delineating objective network characteristics was carried out by Mitchell (1969). He felt that social networks had two basic properties: morphological and interactional. Later attempts at definition of critical dimensions of social networks have followed this tradition. For example, Granovetter (1973) used a similiar method in an attempt to associate specific network content with predictable interactional properties. For networks containing at least three members, Laumann was able to identify two basic typologies of network structure: (a) **Radial** -- self has dyadic relations with members, but members do not interact with each other; (b) **Interlocking** -- self has dyadic relations with members, and at least two members interact with each other.

Mitchell's (1969) original listing of critical social network dimensions has been modified in recent theoretical analysis of networks. The most salient synopsis of network analysis is reported by Jackson, Fischer, and Jones (1977). Emphasis has been placed, in the past, on identifying measures of the structure of networks at the expense of describing the relational content of social networks. for example, one attribute of networks has been labeled "multiplexity". Frankenberg (1966) points out that this indicator has been used in two different ways in network research: (a) to mean the number of different role relations two people have with each other, or (b) to mean the number of contents in a relation such as information and norms of behavior. The former meaning of "multiplexity" is the more commonly used in network research; however, the usage of the term as an empirical indicator remains unclear. A specification of exhaustive "multiplex" categories does not exist and an empirically derived weighting scheme of network relational content categories have not been developed.

Jackson, Fischer, and Jones (1977) compiled a

12

listing of critical network indicators based on their review of the pertinent literature. Whereas Mitchell (1969) made a distinction between structure and function, i.e., morphological vs. interactional, Jackson, Fischer, and Jones (1977) made a conceptual distinction between levels of network analysis. They explicitly distinguish characteristics of different levels of network linkages, i.e., dyadic relations, versus network relations:

1. Dyadic Measures
   a. intimacy -- reported emotional closeness
   b. frequency of contact
   c. duration of the relationship
   d. Role multiplexity -- number of role relations
   e. attributed source of membership -- social context of interaction (family, friend, co-worker, etc.)

2. Network Measures
   a. density -- number of relations/number of possible relations
   b. homogeneity -- ethnic, occupational similiarity, race
   c. dispersion -- range of attributed sources
   d. dominant source -- the modal context of interactions

In summary, the structural analysis of social networks does not show a consistent approach to operationalization in the literature. One problem has been the failure of researchers to clearly specify the relationship between network structure and the function which these networks serve. Aside from the distinction of structure and function, another analytical approach that has been used in social network research is the examination of the relationship of network functions to other variables, such as effective states (Weiss, 1969).

Social Network Functions

Different structural segments of social networks are correlated with specific functions served by the complete network: different segments performed

13

different functions. A person's social network may be divided into several structural segments according to the role relations a person has with network members. A person's relationship to society is multi-faceted and is separated into several categories of role relations. Frankenberg (1969:249) delineates five sets of role relations: (a) kinship and ethnic, (b) economic, (c) political, (d) religious, and (e) recreational. These role relations sets serve as sources of membership for a social network. Social networks emerge as informal social systems which mediate interaction between the individual and society. These networks are composed of members drawn from these formal and informal sets of role relations. Social networks are informal in this sense because membership in a social network is usually a matter of personal choice. Also, participation in a social network is not necessarily determined by performance of institutionalized social roles.

Weiss (1969) echoes the point that multiple network structures provide a differentiated mechanism by which society may shape a person's thinking and acting. A person may receive his or her understanding of social networks, perhaps to a greater degree than from formal educational and work organization. While Frankenberg (1969) categorizes social networks according to structural properties, Weiss (1969) categorizes social networks in terms of relational function. These network segments, which sometimes overlap and are entwined with each other, serve functions of (a) intimacy, (b) social integration, (c) opportunity for nurturant behavior, (d) reassurance of worth, and (e) provision of service (Weiss, 1969:38-40). Failure of a person's social network to serve these functions may have adverse effects on a person's psychological functioning within the context of a specific relationship.

This research assumes that social networks, as informal social structures, provide an individual with consensual definitions of appropriate behavior. The marital relationship serves the function of intimacy within the context of a person's social network. The structure of a person's social network may be expected to impact upon and influence the patterns of behavior found in the marital relationship. The structure and function of social networks are closely related, and behavior in one portion of a network that may be influenced by the structure or function of another are

14

(Weiss 1969, 1974). For example, difficulties with work relationships may effect the marital relationship. (See Figure 1.) In short, the structure and function of a person's social network are related. They are related in the sense that different structures, i.e., portions of the network identified in terms of role relations or communication patterns, may differentially fulfill specific functions for a person. For example, friends, and their associated patterns of communication, may fulfill the advice and information provision function, where spouse and family may fulfill the function of intimacy.

Social Network and Social Support Network: Structure and Function

There is a difference between a person's social network and a person's social support network. The structure of a person's volitional social network (based on a range of membership reservoirs) and a person's social support network are not necessarily coterminous. Social support maybe derived from some members of the network but not from all of the members. Social support is a specific type of interaction, characterized by emotional communication, which is self oriented, constructive in evaluative content, empathetic, and non-judgmental. Social support is the provision of information which tells a person that she/he is valued and belongs to a function network based on perceived commitment of reciprocity and exchange (Cobb, 1976). Social support networks function to: (a) maintain social identity, (b) provide emotional support, (c) provide mutual aid and services, (d) provide access to information, and (e) provide access to new social roles and contacts (Warren, 1976). From this functional description, it can be seen that it is helpful to draw a distinction between instrumental and expressive support. A substantial amount of communication which occurs within social networks maybe characterized as instrumental (child care, legal advice, etc.) rather than emotionally supportive. Role relations based on instrumental exchange are a necessary, but not sufficient condition of the formation of emotional or expressive relationships within social networks (Fischer, 1976:117). The modified Venn diagram, shown in Figure 2, illustrates the fact that the distinguishing characteristic between social networks

15

and social support networks is the relatively high proportion of emotional communication that occurs in the later. A broad definition of social support networks includes the presence of instrumental communication and activities. A narrow definition is confined to the area of a network in which emotional, or affective, communication occurs. The research literature which has investigated social networks often confuses or combines both the broad and narrow definition of social support. The narrower definition of social support networks will be used in this research: Social support is viewed as emotional support based on expressive behavior.

In summary, two points emerge from this review of the network literature: (a) a lack of consensus exists with respect to critical measures of social networks that may predict human behavior; and (b) uniform operational definition of network measures does not exist.

The Relationship Between Social Networks and Patterns of Marital Interaction

The relationship between how a person is enmeshed in his/her social structure and the psychological state of that person is most evident within the field of family therapy. Family therapy, or it's predecessor marital therapy, is built upon the clinical assumption that an etiological linkage exists between a person's social world and their psychological functioning. For example, Mendell, et.al. (1958) state:

> When the individual comes to the therapist for help, we assume that he is admitting failure of his group as an effective milieu in which to find the solution he seeks... Our data suggests that the individual seeking help frequently approaches the therapist to protest against the ineffectiveness of the group to which he belongs.

The step from this statement to analysis of social networks and marital interaction comes with the realization that a person's spouse is a central figure in their social support network. Generally, the spouse is structurally closest to the network focal person and functionally the spouse provides affective intimacy.

16

Another line of inquiry points to the importance of the social networks in determining patterns of interaction within marriage. Lewin's (1935) statement of field theory posits that each person exists within a 'field' of relationships and that each person in this field exerts an influence on the behavior of the focal person. A person's behavior is seen as a product of two forces; psychological structure and social field characteristics. Furthermore, interaction in one part of the field can be influenced by interaction in another part.

Psychological Affects Associated with Interaction Between Spouses

The literature indicates that there are many psychological affects associated with interaction between spouses, for example, love, anger, jealousy, anxiety, hostility, and compassion. However, certain psychological affects may be generated by interaction between spouses (Slater, 1961:269). The interest in this study is based upon affects that result directly from spousal interaction and not the measures of stable affective traits.

Slater (1961) states that anxiety results when one marital partner perceives the other to be withdrawing or disengaging from marital interaction. The person becomes anxious about the condition of the relationship. Uncertainty about the degree of interspousal commitment to the marital relationship, in general, gives rise to anxiety. This anxiety becomes evident when the issue of commitment is increased in salience, such as during marital interaction. For example, a failure to satisfy one spouse's expressive demands may be perceived as a signal of withdrawal by the other spouse.

A social interactional theory of emotions also appears to offer a cogent theoretical explanation of the linkage of patterns of interaction to specific affective states. Kemper (1978) has proposed a structural theory of emotions in which specific emotional states may be predicted from an analysis of the pattern of interaction among any two social actors. The salient point of Kemper's (1978) theory is that negative emotional states (anxiety, hostility) are produced because of a person's perception of inequitable power and status exchanges. In other

17

words, if the perceived characteristics of the power and status relations of two people are known, the presence of a specific emotional state in each may be predicted.

Either excesses or deficiencies of power and status may produce negative emotional states. Kemper (1978) begins his theoretical development with a review of the physiology of emotions and concludes that the two basic affective states associated with social interaction are anxiety and hostility. Kemper (1978) views the lack of satisfaction of expressed demands as characteristic of inequitable marital interaction. This inequity may be seen as a structural deficiency in the marriage and results in the production of anxiety and hostility. Further, hostility may either be directed toward the spouse or towards self, dependent upon who is perceived as not satisfying expressive demands. Hostility outward results when self perceives other as the agent of inequity. Hostility toward self results when the casual agent is perceived as self. Based upon these analyses, this study will focus upon the specific affects of anxiety and hostility.

Summary of Theoretical Perspective

In summary, the theoretical perspective employed in the study is that the presence of intimate and emotionally based social bonds are a prerequisite for adaptable psychological functioning. These intimate and emotional bonds are provided within the structural context of social support networks. Social networks are seen as serving many functions for the individual, affective social support being a functional alternative, which is most closely related to marital interaction.

Social networks are structured so that social support may be provided to a person within different portions of the network. Demarcations between segments of a person's social network may be made in terms of sets of different role relations; for example, the familial as compared to the occupational role segments of a network. All of these network segments interact and overlap and jointly produce an effect that influences a person's behavior. A person's spouse is structurally central to his/her social network. The pattern of interaction is one part of a network may

18

mpact on interaction in another part of the network. t is assumed here that interaction with friends and o-workers, for example, could affect a marital elationship. Conversely, the pattern of interaction ithin the marital relationship could influence a erson's behavior in another portion of his/her etwork. From a clinical perspective, help seeking ehavior is seen as a tacit admission of the failure of person's social network to provide required solutions o problems and needs. The failure to satisfy expressive demands within he marital relationship may result in the generation f anxiety and hostility under certain circumstances. his anxiety and hostility may either be exacerbated or ttenuated dependent upon the characteristics of a erson's social network. In general, loss of multi-aceted social support, from either intimates or other etwork members, may result in psychological discomfort hich is manifested in terms of anxiety and hostility ffects. Lack of social support, in either social phere, will likely yield the same result: generation f psychological discomfort, manifested by expression f anxiety and hostility.

Synopsis of Bott's Study

The most notable study of the relationship between ocial networks and patterns of marital interaction is he qualitative study conducted by Elizabeth Bott 1957). Bott's (1957:ix) study of urban, working class amilies was initially conceived to study family ocial relations and non-political ideology. The esearch was undertaken from a social psychological erspective, and the ultimate goal was the development f hypotheses concerning the association of social rganization (social networks) of the family members to he psychological functioning of family members. The ata collection technique combined participant bservation, sociometric questionnaires, and clinical nterviews. Bott's (1957:15) sample consisted of 20 nglish families, selected from an initial group of 45 hich represented a non-clinical population.
Bott (1957:60) advanced two separate hypothesis fter qualitative analysis of her data: (a) the degree f segregation in the role relationship of husband and ife varies directly with the connectedness of family's ocial network, and (b) the amount of expressive

19

demands made by spouses upon each other is inversely related to the amount of expressive interaction they each have outside the marital relationship. Bott (1957:230) does not offer specific evidence to support either hypothesis and states only a general conclusion:

> "...one of the factors affecting variations in degree of conjugal segregation is the pattern of relationships maintained by members of the family with external people and the relationships of these external people with one another."

Bott concluded that the more friends husband and wife have in common, the more they tend to segregate, or separate, their instrumental roles in the family. As consensual definition of appropriate role behavior increases, through high network interactional density, role behavior becomes more compartmentalized and segregated.

Bott's conclusions regarding the segregation of expressive role behaviors are not very clear cut. A close reading of Bott's (1957) work indicates that expressive role behavior is affected by expectations of both spouses. In the case of Bott's sample, time bound social norms dictated that women should obtain social support from a kinship based network (mother and female friends) and husbands were expected to have a lesser need for social support outside of the marital relationship. Bott found that it was permitted to obtain social support outside the marital relationship is no negative impact was seen on the performance of the husband's instrumental role.

Limited data collection methodology restricted the analysis done by Bott (1957:235) and members of her research team. Specifically, social network data were not collected in an uniformly systematic manner and, in some instances, did not include questions concerning the frequency of contact, nature of relationship, and communication patterns between subjects and network members. The study viewed the family as the unit of analysis; an approach which sacrificed the analytical distinction between the overall family network and the separate networks of husband and wife. Thus, specific discrimination of connections "within" and "between" the two spouses' social network was not always possible. Lastly, the data concerning the psychological impact of network resource upon the marital relationship were gathered by clinical interview and were qualitative rather in quantitative. The focus of the present study is upon elaboration of Bott's second hypothesis, which deals with the differential provision of social support, between spouse and others, and the impact of this provision social support upon the marital relationship. In the discussion of her results, Bott (1957) did identify three sources of variance in the provision of social support: husband's network, wife's network, and husband-wife interaction. The major weakness in Bott's (1957) analysis was the failure to examine all three sources of variation. A more complete picture of the relationship between network structure and the psychological affects associated with interaction between spouses can only be derived from a concurrent analysis of husband's network structure, wife's network structure, and specific affective outcome of marital interaction.

The network perspective presented here is an elaboration of Bott's second hypothesis, which further specifies the effects of the structural properties of spousal and couple networks. Figure 3 illustrates the fact that spouses each have a social network with distinct boundaries and, at the same time, these individual networks overlap. This overlapping, or interconnections in Bott's terminology, allows for interaction of each spouse's network with the other. This is an elaboration of Bott's basic model in that it shows the indirect effects through interaction of each spouse's network upon the other spouse and the effects of network interconnections.

Recent Research Findings

Examinations of Bott's (1957) first hypothesis, which deals with instrumental role segregation, have been carried out by several researchers. Aldous and Strauss (1966) attempted a partial test of the hypothesis by investigating structural factors which were related to the "degree of network connectedness." Dichotomous categories of socioeconomic status (high/low) and residential location (urban/non-urban) served as independent variables in the analysis. Aldous and Strauss (1966) were unable to find clear cut, significant patterns in their data which would lend support to the Bott hypothesis. However, they

FIGURE 3

Properties of Married Couple Social Network

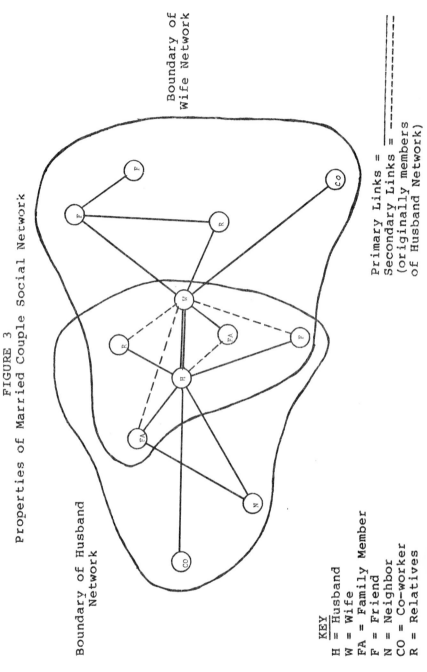

Boundary of Husband
Network

Boundary of
Wife Network

KEY
H = Husband
W = Wife
FA = Family Member
F = Friend
N = Neighbor
CO = Co-worker
R = Relatives

Primary Links = _____
Secondary Links = -----------
(originally members
of Husband Network)

22

note that a lack of data on the structure of husband's social network may have biased their results. An explanation of this lack of adequate data is not provided.

Turner (1967) re-examined Bott's first hypothesis. Turner attempted to relate network connectedness between husband and wife with marital role tasks, such as child care, household chores, and other factors such as occupation, geographical mobility, educational level, stage of development cycle, and cosmopolitan or local orientation. After citing methodological problems, Turner (1967:129), reported that his results were inconclusive.

Toomey (1971) prepared a synopsis of studies that have investigated both of Bott's (1957) hypotheses. Studies aimed at an examination of Bott's first hypothesis, dealing with instrumental role segregation, largely contain negative results, e.g., Udry and Hall (1961), Aldous and Strauss (1966), and Harrel-Bond (1969). This second set of studies has "relied upon measures of the socio-emotional nature of married relationships" (Toomey, 1971:418). Thus, studies which are directed at a replication of Bott's first hypothesis appear to have negative results, whereas studies which purport to test the second hypothesis have demonstrated moderate support.

However, Toomey (1971) notes that his own analysis, based on a sample of 206 wives and 180 husbands (some of whom were not married to each other), appears to support similiar findings by Nelson (1966) that marital partner interaction and extramarital social networks act as alternative sources of emotional support. Nelson's (1966) work, which is directly related to Bott's second hypothesis, indicates that spouses may seek emotional support from members of their network in cases where they are not provided support by their spouses. Having a network which is capable of providing this emotional support lessens the demand made upon the spouse. This conClusion is also supported in a comprehensive review of the literature on family interaction patterns, in which Aldous (1977) cites evidence that suggests connections between individual spouse networks are an important explanatory variable in pedicting marital behavior. Aldous cites Ramey (1975), who notes that his research on intimate friendships indicates that extramarital friendship may remove some of the emotional pressure from the marital relation while increasing the partner's range of experiences.

This brief review of the literature presents inconsistent results in the testing of Bott's (1957) hypotheses. These inconsistencies appear to be due to two factors: (a) failure to separate, clearly and analytically, instrumental and expressive character- istics of social networks as they relateto marital interaction patterns, and (b) failure to consider simultaneously both individual and joint characteris- tics of social networks as they relate to psychological affects associated with marital interaction. Thus, further investigation of the relationship between the structure of social networks and affects associated with marital interaction is warranted.

Identification of Network Characteristics

The previous discussion of social networks showed that they may be described by a wide range of indicators. In addition, a conceptual distinction between social networks and social support networks allows a focus upon specific dimensions of networks as they relate to affects associated with marital interaction. In the bulk of past research, expressive and instrumental functions have been combined during operationalization. This failure, as noted earlier, has in part prevented a thorough examination of Bott's second hypothesis.

Identification of specific variables which may be significantly related to variation in affects associated with marital interaction comes through an examination of theoretical discussions, previous research and the specific context of this study. One consistent thread that flows through discussion of social networks, as they influence behavior, is the effect of size of network upon social actors. From the theoretical formulations of Simmel (1908) to the recent work of Pattison (1975), size of network may be identified as an important variable.

Bott's (1957) study focused on the connections between social networks. In several other studies, this has been translated to mean the number of shared friends between husband and wife. Here, this variable will be called the degree of inter-connectedness between networks. The literature also indicates that density of networks (Fischer, 1977:36) may be associated with the effect of network has upon a person. Translating this into the study context, it becomes necessary to consider the degree to which members of a specific social network interact with one another, independently of the network focal person. this variable will be called density and refers to communicative connections within a specific network.

In order to develop a clear understanding of the hypothesized relationship between social support and affects associated with marital interaction, it is necessary to measure the amount of expressive or emotional communication which take place within a person's social network. One aspect of social support is "emotional support" or the amount of communications between people which is devoted to discussions about feelings and emotions (Cobb, 1976).

In the present context, the focal variable will be the amount of communication between a person and network members which is devoted to talk about feelings and emotions. This network indicator will be called amount of emotional communication and is assumed to be a reflection of the intimacy of the network linkages. Summation of these individual linkage contents will yield an indicator of the total amount of emotional communcation in the network. Closely related to the content of communication is the frequency at which this communication occurs. Frequency of communication may be combined with content to deduce relative quantities of supportive communication which occurs across different sources of network membership.

The source of membership in a person's network may be an important variable in network analysis as indicated by the work by Jackson, Fischer and Jones (1977). Source and network membership is taken as an indirect indicator of social role and is expected to reflect the salience of network linkages to the social actor. For example, the specific social support function is expected to vary across differing social contexts, such as occupationally based relationships, as opposed to kinship based network linkages (Weiss, 1969) (See Figure 1). Therefore source of membership will be included in the analysis and allows an examination of the effect source of membership has upon psychological affects associated with marital interaction. The inclusion of this variable provides a linkage between the structural and functional analysis of social networks.

Variation in network characteristics can be expected to influence psychological affects. It is

25

difficult to specify the exact nature of these relationships at this time; the general goal in this research is the further specification of these variable relationships. However, the literature suggests that networks should be of sufficient size, interconnected, dense, provide substantial emotional communication and have members recruited from a range of sources in order to provide individuals with a satisfactory amount of relational support. Weiss (1969) summarizes this view by stating that it is difficult to specify which of the relational functions, provided by social networks, are more important than others in maintaining emotional stability within the context of marital interaction.

Six specific indicators of network structure have been identified, which may be related to affects associated with marital interaction. These indicators are network size, density, interconnectedness, amount of emotional communication, frequency of communication, and source of network membership. The review of the literature associated with Bott's (1957) hypotheses suggests that network indicators, either singularly or in combination, bay be critical variables with respect to variance in affects associated with marital interaction.

The Research Question

Given the context of this study, the research problem may now be rephrased in the form of two hypotheses, as follows:

(1) The level of anxiety and hostility associated with marital interaction is inversely related with the variation in the following: (a) social network size, (b) density of social network, (c) interconnection with social network of spouse, and (d) amount of emotional communication.

(2) There is a positive relationship between frequency of communication and categories of relationship, method and kind of communication arranged by descending orders of intimacy as stated by Weiss (1969).

CHAPTER 3

METHODOLOGY

The context of this study is the solution of a ractical problem posed within the field of nterpersonal relations. The data available for nalysis were collected primarily for purposes other han investigation of the present research question. herefore, examination of the research question has een limited by the secondary nature of the data nalysis.

Subjects

A group of eight married couples (16 persons) erved as subjects in the research. The average age as 35 years; for wives, 33 years. On the average, he couples had been married for 13 years and had two hildren. Average family income was $31,000 annually; hree wives were not employed outside the home. Both embers of three couples were employed in professional ccupations, e.g., education and nursing. The emainder of the subjects held various sales, anagerial, and clerical jobs. All subjects were creened through psychiatric interviews prior to their oluntary participation in the research program. The ubjects were assessed as being members of a non-linical population. From a demographic perspective, he sample was a homogeneous middle class, urban group. ubjects expected to benefit from their participation n the research project through enhanced self-onfidence, increased emotional insight, improved nterpersonal communication, greater ability to express eelings, and improved coping abilities.

Operationalization of Theoretical Concepts

Two sets of indicators are employed: network characteristics and measures of psychological affects associated with interaction between spouses. The indicators of social network structure are size, interconnections between spouse networks, density, amount of emotional communication, and frequency of communication. In addition, source of membership for network members is included in the analysis. Psychological affects associated with interaction between spouses are indicated by levels of anxiety and hostility present during marital interaction.

Size of network is a measure of the number of people in one's self reported network. Degree of interconnection is a ration of the number of existing interconnections between husband and wife networks to the number of persons in both networks. Existing interconnections are the number of persons cited by both spouses as being members of their respective networks. This indicator is derived from a coding scheme where numbering of networks entries is standardized on one spouse.

Density of networks is a calculated measure based upon a formula developed by Turner (1967:122). Density of a network is a ratio of the number of people within the network who know each other, including subject, to the maximum number of possible connections between people in the network. The number of people within the network who know each other is taken from information provided by the subject. The maximum number of possible interconnections is: $n(n-1)/2$, where $n =$ total number of persons in the network. Density would equal 1.00 if everyone in the network communicated with everyone else in the network, and if there were no communication at all between network members, the density would equal zero.

The amount of emotional communication which occurs between a subject and his/her social network members is the product of the proportion of communication devoted to emotional issues multiplied by an index of frequency of communication. The amount of emotional communication which occurs between subject and any one member of the network may be calculated from self-reported indices of network structure. An approximate measure of the amount of communication devoted to emotional topics as compared to other types of possible communication, i.e., communication about emotions,

28

ideas, things, or other people. This proportion may range from 0% to 100% (0.0 to 1.00).

Frequency of communication was measured on the ordinal scale of 1 to 7. Maximum frequency of communication (7) would be self-reports of more than one communicative act per day; (0) would be self-reports of communication less than once a year. For each individual link in the subject's social network a measureof amount of emotional communication of emotional communication and frequency of communication. A summary measure of emotional communication which was used in the analysis has been calculated by summing these individual indicators over all network entries.

Source of membership for network members is measured on a nominal scale indicating the nature of the role relationship between subject and network members. Categories of spouse, immediate family members (parents, children), relatives, friends neighbor (residential closeness), and co-workers were used as measures of source of network membership. Measures of anxiety and hostility experienced during marital interaction were used as indicators of psychological affects associated with interaction between spouses.

Procedures

Instruments

The instruments used to gather data concerning the social networks of subjects was an expanded modification of a projected psychometric instrument called the Personal Sphere Model Test (PSM) developed by Schmeideck (1978). This instrument, originally developed to aid in clinical diagnosis, has been based on principles of Jungian psychology, in which the subjective relationship of self to others is an important clinical indicator of mental disorder. The modification made here has been carried out to aid in the development of behavioral indicators of a person's relationship to the members of his or her own network. The PSM is designed to be administered in a nonreactive fashion; instructions for completion are contained within the test. The PSM was administered on an individual basis without the presence of an interviewer. A copy of the instrument is attached as Appendix A.

29

The basic modification made to the PSM has bee
the addition of a descriptive matrix which measure
communication between the test subject and members o
his/her social network. The matrix was constructed o
the basis of a review of other instruments used t
measure the structure of social networks, e.g.
Pattison (1975). For each person identified in th
projective portion of the test, subjects are require
to state, in categorical terms, their relationship t
the person, frequency, method, and type o
communication with that person, and data indicative o
who communicates with whom within the network. Thi
procedure yields five self-reported behaviora
indicators of dyadic links between a subject and up t
20 other persons. A maximum of a 5 by 20 cell matri
is thus generated which describes behavioral pattern
of communication between all persons, includin
subject, in the target social network. The modifie
PSM has been pretested on a sample of 45 colleg
undergraduates to eliminate problems of clarity in th
instructions, structure of the test, and ease o
administration.

The levels of anxiety and hostility for marita
partners were assessed by use of a modified version o
the Free Association Test (FAT) (Gottschalk and Gleser
1969). FAT scores are derived from the conten
analysis of a typescript constructed from a five-to
seven minute tape recording in which subjects ar
instructed to talk about personal experience
reflective of feelings. Typescripts are evaluated fo
specific types of anxiety (Death, Mutilation
Separation, Guilt, Shame, and Diffuse) and hostilit
(Outward Overt, Outward Covert, Inward, an
Ambivalent). Scores for the six types of anxiety ar
combined into a summary measure reflecting the Tota
Anxiety indicated in the typescript. Summary measure
for Total Hostility Outward and Total Hostility Inwar
and Ambivalent are obtained in a similar manner. Fo
all variables scores are corrected for the total numbe
of words spoken. Further description of the FAT i
given in Silbergeld, Manderscheid, and O'Neill (1975).

Silbergeld and Manderscheid (1976) report use of
Dyadic Free Association Test (DFAT) and note tha
presence of marital partner is likely to increase th
levels of anxiety and hostility, as compared to level
found in the individual FAT. The DFAT differs from th
FAT in that transcripts are recorded for a period of 1
to 12 minutes when spouses are engaged in conversatio

with each other. Therefore, indicators may be developed which measure the amount of contribution each spouse makes to the total DFAT scores. The content analysis protocols for scoring DFAT's are the same as those used for the FAT, as is the basic method of calculating scores and summary measures. This research will utilize summary measures of anxiety and hostility taken from the DFAT.

Method of Data Collection

Prior to participating in brief group psychotherapy for married couples, research subjects complete a series of orientation, screening, summary, and interim sessions. The purpose of these sessions is to assess couple qualifications and mutual desirability, to take comprehensive, individual spouse psychiatric histories, and to provide interim contact with clinical staff before beginning the brief group psychotherapy. Prior to and following each of seven consecutive interim sessions a five-to-seven minute individual FAT is completed, and followed by a ten-to-twelve minute DFAT. At the conclusion of this seven interview series subjects complete the Personal Sphere Model (PSM) Questionnaire. All data to be utilized in this research have been collected prior to the beginning of brief group psychotherapy for the couples.

Analysis of Data

Coding/Data Reduction

All data were coded, keypunched, and stored on tape to facilitate computer analysis. A codebook for the PSM instrument was developed and revised to meet the requirements of the research problem. Custom FORTRAN programs were written to facilitate the complex analysis of the social network matrices. Prepared data analytical computer package, such as Biomedical Data Program (BMDP) (Brown, 1977) and the Statistical Analysis System (SAS) (SAS, 1979) were used to analyze the data. Computer facilities of the Public Health Service were used for data analysis.

31

DFAT Index Construction

A unique feature of this research is the use of very discrete affect indicators and dependent variables. A complex procedure that has been used to collect measures of psychological affects associated with interaction between spouses poses both analytical problems and advantages. No construction of an index based on a set of seven repeated measures complicates the analysis. However, the advantage of this procedure is the statistical control of individual variation over time, including differential reactivity to data collection, may be exercised. Each of these possible contaminating effects maybe removed from anxiety/hostility levels by using techniques of computing mean scores for the seven session scores. Differential reactivity to data collection, or anticipation of contact with clinical staff, is controlled by subtracting pre-session DFAT scores from post session DFAT scores prior to session averaging. In summary, the anxiety/hostility levels used in the analysis were adjusted for variation associated with differential scores across time and possible reactive effects of the data collection procedure.

Two major tasks were accomplished during the data analysis in order to fully explore the research question: (a) association of network indicators with anxiety/hostility levels for both husband and wife and (b) association of frequency of communication with source of membership, method and kind of communication taken in descending orders of intimacy. Each data analytic task, (a) and (b) above, was accomplished through a series of separate analyses described below.

Research Hypothesis 1: An inverse relationship exists between network size, density, interconnection and other social networks, frequency of emotional communication, and anxiety/hostility levels associated with marital interaction. A series of multiple regression analyses were carried out in which the dependent variables of anxiety/hostility were regressed upon network indicators (size, density, etc.). Separate analyses were conducted for husband network indicators, wife network indicators, anxiety as the dependent variable, and hostility as the dependent variable.

Research Hypothesis 2: A positive relationship exists between frequency of communication and categories of relationship (source of network membership), method, and kind of communication arranged in descending orders of intimacy. In descending order of intimacy the categories of role relationship are spouse, family, relatives, friends, neighbors, and co-workers. An analysis of variance, in which only main effects were examined, was conducted to examine this hypothesis.

Limitations

One major data analytic constraint usually encountered is research on social networks is sample size. The conclusions drawn from this study are therefore limited by the size of the sample used. Statistical description of variable relationships are presented as heuristic aids in interpretation of the data. Statements of statistical significance are not intended as statements of generality of these results. However, two points counter the methodological problems posed by small sample size. First, the analysis is exploratory in nature, and it is not intended that inferences will be made from this sample to a population. Second, the research centers on the examination of a specific social structure (i.e., social networks) as it relates to specific psychological affects in interpersonal interaction. The use of discrete affect indicators and a very homogeneous study sample counteracts these limitations.

The basic nature of this study presents certain limitations to the use of the results. The excellent reviews of the network literature provided by Henderson (1980) and Mueller (1980) both indicate the dependent variable indicators with the specificity and physiological validity of the FAT have not been employed in research centered on social networks. Therefore, the findings presented must be viewed in the on text of the use of these dependent variable measures. It may be that these results, reported below, have never been found because techniques for assessing affect variation never existed to the degree of specificity employed in this study.

Another caveat usually applied to network studies is the variation in network effect may be a function of geographic location, social class position and other ecological variables. These effect have been negated in this study by careful sample selection. There is no variability across these cogent structural indicators in this sample. This homogeneity allows the drawing of conclusions which might otherwise be suspect given the sample size employed. It is not necessary to 'statistically' control for these effects in the analysis. Sample sizes of 100 or more might yield a smaller effective sample if variation of social class, residence and other variables were 'partialled out' of the analyses.

Finally, these results are limited by the intended application. This study was intended to serve as a guidepost for further investigations; not as a definitive work on the relationship of social structure to the generation of affect. This study generates hypotheses for future testing. These hypotheses are outlined in broad strokes in the final chapter.

CHAPTER 4

FINDINGS

This chapter reports the results of the analysis described in the preceeding chapter. A statistical description of all variables included in the analysis is presented and is followed with presentation of significant findings. Only those results which displayed statistical and substantive significance are reported here, additional results and supplementary data are contained in Appendix C.

Table 1

Means and Standard Deviations for Study Variable

	Statistical Analysis	
Variable 1,2,3	Mean	Standard Deviation
NTER	3.375	2.560
NTRA1H	0.156	0.098
NTRA2H	0.294	0.129
NTRA3H	0.144	0.170
REQH	0.726	0.336
KZEH	14.625	4.173
NTRA1W	0.133	0.109
NTRA2W	0.179	0.126
NTRA3W	0.184	0.123
REQW	0.746	0.182
KZEW	13.625	3.420

Descriptions of the Sample Variables

Variable 1,2,3	Statistical Analysis	
	Mean	Standard Deviation
HC7P (ANX)	1.706	0.457
HC10P (HOT)	1.160	0.424
HC13P (HIA)	0.729	0.267
WC7P (ANX)	1.660	0.507
WC10P (HOT)	1.080	0.311
WC13P (HIA)	0.911	0.236

[1]
 H = husband; W = wife.
[2]
 C7P = total anxiety; C10P = total hostility outward;
 C13P = hostility inward and ambivalent.
[3]
 N = 16 for INTER; in all other cases N = 8.

Table 1 displays the means and standard deviations
for all variables included in the regression analyses.
The variables which are labeled "INTRA" are measures of
network density. The review of the social network
literature contained in Chapter II suggests that
density of social networks is normally calculated by a
single method that was developed by Turner (1967:122).
This method is cited in most empirical research on
social networks which has employed density measures.
Due to the exploratory nature of this investigation,
several alternative methods of calculating density were
included in the data analysis. This was done because
it appears that the traditional method of calculating
density does not necessarily capture all the effects
social networks have upon the subject members. In
order to elucidate the variable impacts of density
considered in the present study, the method employed to
calculate the density measures is outlined as follows.
    Given a social network which includes a research
subject (SELF) and five other people (A, B, C, D, E)
the following relationships are assumed:

36

```
A knows B
B knows A
C knows B
D knows E
E knows D
```

Diagraming these relationships we have:

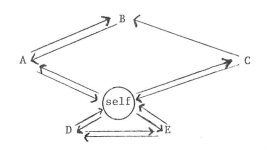

Three network density measures may now be calculated at follows:

Density 1 (INTRA 1):   The number of people who have reciprocal knowledge of each other, excluding relationships with network subject (SELF). Links between (A, B) and (D,E) are reciprocal; thus <u>INTRA 1 would be "2"</u>.

Density 2 (INTRA 2):   The number of people who have reciprocal knowledge of each other, including relationships within network subject (SELF). Links between (A, B) and (D, E) and all links between SELF and others; thus, <u>INTRA 2 would be "6"</u>.

Density 3 (INTRA 3):   The number of people who have unidirectional; relationships within the network. The link between C and B is unidirectional; thus, <u>INTRA 3 would be "1"</u>.

In the research reported here, each of thes[e] calculations was made for every subject's socia[l] network. In addition, these density measures wer[e] standardized so comparisons could be made acros[s] networks on different sizes.

Table 2

Correlation Matrix for Independent Variables
by Marital Role

Husband (N=8)	Wife					
	INTRA1	INTRA2	INTRA3	INTER	SIZE	FREQ
INTRA1	+.32 (.43)	+.24 (.55)	-.52 (.18)	-.19 (.64)	+.04 (.90)	+.89 (.002)
INTRA2	+.50 (.19)	+.42 (.29)	-.67 (.06)	-.25 (.53)	-.01 (.97)	+.89 (.002)
INTRA3	+.58 (.12)	+.75 (.03)	-.28 (.49)	-.22 (.59)	-.67 (.06)	+.04 (.90)
INTER	+.01 (.98)	-.09 (.83)	-.003 (.99(	1.000 1.000	+.42 (.29)	-.53 (.17)
SIZE	-.78 (.02)	-.74 (.03)	+.81 (.01)	+.32 (.43)	+.22 (.58)	-.65 (.08)
FREQ.	+.52 (.18)	+.56 (.14)	-.66 (.06)	-.22 (.59)	-.33 (.41)	+.79 (.01)

1
Probability levels enclosed in parentheses are below corresponding Pearson correlations.

Correlation of Independent and Dependent Variables

Table 2 displays the correlation matrix for the independent variables used in the regression analyses.

These results are interesting for two reasons: evidence of multicollinearity and relationships between husband and wife network structures. Tables 3 and 4 show the correlation matrices for independent variables for husband and wife networks respectively. Inspection of these tables indicates that interpretation of regression analysis results are complicated by the existence of multicollinearity among the independent variables in the multiple regression equations. Gordon (1968) notes that this probelm of multicollinearity is more closely related to theoretical interpretation than to statistical validity. Blalock (1963) echoes this same point in his discussion of interpretation of standardized regression coefficients in sociological research. To guard against fallacious interpretation of regression results two analytic techniques were employed in this analysis: examination of standard errors of each independent variable; and inspection of individual variable tests of significant contributions (T test) to the overall regression results. In those analyses where standard errors were small compared to regression coefficients (S.E.x1.96 < β) and the individual test of significance met established criteria (p .10), the data were interpreted as being minimally effected by collinearity (Dhrymes, 1978:190). Further, the small sample size itself requires that results be interpreted to allow for the instability of regression coefficients in different samples.

Table 3

Correlation Matrix for Husband Network Indicators (N=8)

	INTER	INTRA1	INTRA2	INTRA3	FREQ	SIZE
INTER	1.000					
INTRA1	-.192	1.000				
INTRA2	-.256	.961*	1.000			
INTRA3	-.224	-.169	-.044	1.000		
FREQ	-.233	.800*	.816*	.373	1.000	
SIZE	.322	-.566	-.566	-.387	-.705*	

*p≥.05.

Examination of Table 2 also indicates that the

characteristics of husband and wife social networks are intercorrelated. For example, frequency of emotional communication in husband network is correlated with frequency of emotional communication in wife network, r=+.79 (p=.01). This fact must be taken into account during the interpretation of the regression analyses results presented below.

Table 5 is a correlation matrix of dependent variables used in the regression analyses. The significant finding in this analysis is that husband and wife anxiety covary, r=+.722 (p=.04). Therefore, any relationship found between individual network structure and anxiety must be viewed within the context of interaction with the affective state of the other spouse. Change in the husband network structure which is associated with lower levels of anxiety may then be linked to the lowering of anxiety in the other spouse.

Table 4

Correlation Matrix for Wife Network Indicators (N=8)

	INTER	INTRA1	INTRA2	INTRA3	FREQ	SIZE
INTER	1.000					
INTRA1	.010	1.000				
INTRA2	-.090	.945*	1.000			
INTRA3	.003	-.845	-.750*	1.000		
FREQ	-.535	.285	.258*	-.403	1.000	
SIZE	.426	-.191	-.494	.052	-.103	1.000

*p$\geq$.05.

Conversely, variation in network structure associated with a rise in anxiety of one spouse may be linked to an increase of anxiety in the other spouse. The result supports the implicit assumption of Bott's (1957) work that there is a linkage between spouse network and affects associated with marital interaction.

Research Hypothesis 1

The significant finding which emerged from the regression analysis was the relationship of husband and

40

wife network characteristics to variation in Total
Anxiety levels associated with marital interaction.
The analysis testing the relationship of network
characteristics with Total Hostility Outward and Total
Hostility Inward and Ambivalent did not produce
significant correlations. Regression of wife
anxiety/hostility levels upon husband network
indicators, and the husband affects upon wife network
indicators did not reveal significant results either.

Tables 6 and 7 are the results of regression
analysis of husband network characteristics and anxiety
levels. The combination of independent variables
reported are the most parsimonious combinations.
Tables 6 and 7 differ in the respect that different
sets of network density descriptors were included in
the analysis. An inspection of these tables
illustrates the effect that differing
conceptualizations of density have upon affects. For
example, the inclusion of Density(2) and Density(3) as
compared to Density(1) and Density(3) changes the beta
of SIZE from +.402 to -.518. This suggests that
network density effect is very complex and cannot be
captured by using of a single network density
indicator.

Table 5

Correlation Matrix for Dependent Variables
Anxiety, Hostility Outward,
Hostility Inward and Ambivalent

| Husband (N = 8) | Wife (N = 8) | | |
	ANX[1]	HOT	HIA
ANX	+.722 (.04)	-.29 (.47)	+.37 (.36)
HOT	+.386 (.34)	+.560 (.14)	+.58 (.12)
HIA	+.086 (.83)	+.36 (.36)	-.45 (.26)

1
Probability levels enclosed in parentheses are below corresponding Pearson correlations.

In summary, these results indicate that the most cogent effect of network structure upon variation in anxiety is found in a combination of density and frequency of emotional communication. The other variables have a significaNT effect, but the magnitude of density and frequency factors is substantially greater than the others.

Table 6

Husband Network Structure
Predicting Husband Anxiety (Density 1 & 2)

Multiple R	0.9971	F Ratio	69.074
Multiple R-Square	0.9942	P(Tail)	0.01433

Variable	Coefficient	Standard Error	Standard Regression Coefficient	P(2 Tail)
INTERCEPT	2.929			
INTRA1	10.507	0.844	2.247	0.006
INTRA3	3.617	0.322	1.343	0.008
FREQ	-4.010	0.247	-2.947	0.004
SIZE	-0.057	0.009	-0.518	0.024
INTER	0.106	0.011	0.518	0.010

Tables 8 and 9 are the results of regression analyses of wife network indicators and anxiety levels. Again, as in the husband network analysis, differing combinations of density variables were used in the analysis. High multiple correlations are similar to those of husband network indicators (r=.996). Interpretation of these wife network analysis takes on meaning when they are compared to those of the husbands. A comparison of Table 6 to 8 and Table 7 to 9 reveals important analytical results. The major finding of this study is that the relationship of network characteristics to variation in affects associated with marital interaction is different for husbands as compared to wives.

Table 7

Husband Network Structure
Predicting Husband Anxiety (Density 2 & 3)

ultiple R	0.9967	F Ratio	60.161
ultiple R-Square	0.9934	P(Tail)	0.01643

ariable	Coefficient	Standard Error	Standard Regression Coefficient	P(2 Tail)
NTERCEPT	0.089			
NTRA1	8.943	0.770	2.526	0.007
NTRA3	3.438	0.332	1.277	0.009
REQ	-3.454	0.222	-2.537	0.004
IZE	0.044	0.015	0.402	0.094
NTER	0.105	0.011	0.588	0.011

A comparison of the regression in which Density(2)
nd Density(3) were included for husbands and wives
how a striking difference in the effect of FREQUENCY.
or husbands (Table 7), the beta for FREQUENCY is -
2.537 and the beta for wives (Table 9) is +.366. This
ndicates that an increase in emotional communication
or husbands, within their social networks, is
nversely correlated with the total anxiety they
xperience during interaction with their wives.
owever, the observation is true for wives, where an
ncrease in emotional communication is associated with
n increase of anxiety. The result for husbands
orresponds to the predicted result and the results for
ives is opposite of the predicted direction of
ovariation. Therefore, a difference has been
emonstrated in the relationship of network
haracteristics to affects between husbands and wives.
   Noting this finding, an additional series of
egressions were conducted. These additional
egressions pooled the data of husbands and wives in
rder to examine the nature of this gender effect.
nclusion of SEX as a dummy variable in these equations
id not reveal significant results. The structural
haracteristics of the social network of husband and
ife are significantly intercorrelated, preventing a
alid analysis, i.e., multiple regression, of their
ombined networks upon total couple dependent
ariables. However, a combination of husband and wife

43

network indicators does reveal overall relationship (Tables 10 and 11) which approaches significance. These regression models indicate that different variables are linked to the production of Anxiety (Table 10) and Hostility Inward and Ambivalent (Table 11).

Table 8

Wife Network Structure
Predicting Wife Anxiety (Density 1 & 2)

Multiple R	0.9962	F Ratio	52.817
Multiple R-Square	0.9925	P(Tail)	0.1869

Variable	Coefficient	Standard Error	Standard Regression Coefficient	P(2 Tail)
INTERCEPT	-2.083			
INTRA1	7.073	0.563	1.521	0.006
INTRA3	5.854	0.516	1.424	0.008
FREQ	1.044	0.236	0.376	0.048
SIZE	0.036	0.011	0.244	0.079
INTER	0.134	0.017	0.677	0.016

Table 9

Wife Network Structure
Predicting Wife Anxiety (Density 3 & 4)

Multiple R	0.9989	F Ratio	183.105
Multiple R-Square	0.9978	P(Tail)	0.00544

Variable	Coefficient	Standard Error	Standard Regression Coefficient	P(2 Tail)
INTERCEPT	-4.043			
INTRA1	6.726	0.287	1.670	0.002
INTRA3	5.581	0.267	1.358	0.002
FREQ	1.016	0.127	0.366	0.015
SIZE	0.121	0.008	0.817	0.004
INTER	0.118	0.009	0.595	0.006

44

Table 10

Couple Dyad C7P (Anxiety)

Multiple R	0.9831	F Ratio	11.532
Multiple R-Square	0.9665	P(Tail)	0.08171

Variable	Coefficient	Standard Error	Standard Regression Coefficient	P(2 Tail)
INTERCEPT	-2.372			
INTER	0.247	0.042	1.356	0.027
INTRA2H	-3.471	1.560	-0.960	0.156
FREQH	-2.654	0.444	-1.909	0.027
INTRA2W	4.367	0.776	1.177	0.030
FREQW	6.699	1.488	2.616	0.046

In the case of Anxiety and model indicates that Frequency of Emotional Communication for Wife is strongly and positively related to Anxiety. Density-(2)Wife is similarly related to Frequency-Husbands is negatively related at one half the numerical magnitude of Density(2)Wife. As the density and frequency of emotional communication increases for the wife so does the total couple anxiety. This trend is weakly counteracted by increasing the frequency of husband emotional communication. Therefore, the frequency of density of wife's network are clearly associated with the production of couple anxiety.

In the case of Hostility Inward and Ambivalent the model indicates that Frequency-Wife and Density(1)Wife are positively related to production of the couple Hostility Inward and Ambivalent. This trend is balanced very strongly by density (INTRA1H) of husbands network. Therefore, as frequency and density of wife's network increases so does couple hostility inward and ambivalent. This increase is almost exactly balanced by an increase in husband network density. In sum, a comparison indicates that couple affects are more clearly associated with the characteristics of wife's network. In the case of Hostility Inward and Ambivalent, these effects are almost totally counteracted by the husband network density effect.

Table 11

Couple Dyad C13P (Hostility Inward and Ambivalent)

Multiple R	0.9994	F Ratio	135.550
Multiple R-Square	0.9988	P(Tail)	0.06565

Variable	Coefficient	Standard Error	Standard Regression Coefficient	P(2 Tail)
INTERCEPT	-1.827			
INTER	-3.835	0.194	-1.976	0.032
INTRA2H	0.346	0.049	0.612	0.089
FREQH	0.036	0.004	0.799	0.067
INTRA2W	1.568	0.122	0.901	0.050
FREQW	2.181	0.107	2.096	0.031
SIZEW	0.046	0.003	0.833	0.035

Summary of Regression Results

In general, the interrelationship of networ
characteristics is as follows: the larger the network
the less frequent the communication within the networ
and the less dense (INTRA2) the network. However, th
larger the spouse network the more the number o
interconnections there are between spouse network th
more the number of interconnections there are betwee
spouse networks. Although non-significant,
correlation analysis of the combined network
indicators shows that the more highly interconnecte
networks are, the more anxiety is found in coupl
interactions. This finding is contrary to th
predicted relationship. Although some of thes
relationships approach significance (p=.10), they d
not reach the predicted level of p=.05. Table 12 is
display of these combined indicator correlations.

Anxiety is associated primarily with a persons
own network characteristics, especially for women, an
the critical network characteristics are size an
frequency. However, these beneficial network effect
are balanced by the direct effect of a spouses networ
transmitted through degree of interconnection betwee
networks. This positive effect disappears when contac
with spouse network is made and anxiety is generated i

46

proportion to reported contact with common network members.

Table 12

Model Correlations of Combined Network
Structural Indicators (N = 16)

Independent Var.(s)	Dependent Variable	$\overline{R}^2$	P
INTERCONNECTIONS	ANXIETY	+.47	.06
INTRA2 (Density)	FREQUENCY	+.59	.004
INTRA2 (Density)	SIZE	-.61	.006
FREQUENCY	SIZE	-.48	.039
INTERCONNECTIONS	SIZE	+.41	.08

Total hostility outward (HOT) appears to stem from a persons' network and may be reinforced by spouses network size without any interconnections. This finding suggests the role of perception via symbolism as a possible explanatory factor in this relationship. Hostility inward and ambivalent (HIA) is primarily associated with your spouses network and may be reinforced by increased frequency of interaction with subject's network.

In summary, there are interrelation between spousal networks as they relate to affects found during marital interaction. This pattern can generally be described as follows: anxiety is inversely related to a person's network, but his inverse relation is outweighed 2 to 1 by interconnection with spouses network. Spouses network members reinforce anxiety, and it increases at a faster rate than a person's network can balance it.

Hostility outward increases with size and frequency of emotional communication in the network; an increase in hostility outward is associated with decreased importance of spouses network. Hostility inward and ambivalent: outward hostility in spouse increases hostility inward and ambivalence. This is amplified with increased frequency of emotional communication in a persons' network, which in turn, generates hostility outward.

This picture is extremely complex and suggests

47

that beneficial characteristics of one spousal network may be balanced by negative characteristics of the other. The more highly interconnected these networks are, the more profound are these balancing effects. However, the affects of anxiety, hostility outward, and hostility inward are themselves interrelated and occur in a pattern. The intervention which might alleviate anxiety may be the same ones which can produce hostility outward which in turn would generate hostility inward in the other spouse. Also, the intervention which may reduce inward hostility in one spouse may be the same intervention, coupled with high interconnections, which would increase anxiety in the other spouse.

The contextual picture presented by this data is one in which density of network and frequency of emotional communication effect variable relationships in opposite directions. This picture is also different for men and women and varies according to the dependent variable included in the analysis. Therefore, specification of the relationship between network characteristics and affects associated with marital interaction must be subclassified by specific affect, gender of respondent, and method of network density measurement.

In conclusion, the process that relates social support networks to variation in affects associated with marital interaction is different for each dependent variable and sex of subject also has a differential effect of each of the dependent variables. However, the characteristics of the data base, i.e., sample size, and the complexity of the communications patterns (number of cogent descriptors) prevent a more detailed analysis. Therefore, statement of findings can best be expressed as suggestions for further research which would elucidate these results. These results show that social networks are clearly involved in the psychic states of a sample of married persons coping with typical life situations of the urban middle class.

Research Hypothesis 2

The second general research hypothesis stated that significantly different patterns of emotional communication exist across categories of role relationship between subject and members of their social networks. This hypothesis was examined through analysis and variance of frequency of emotional communication within and between categories of relationship (spouse, family, relative, friend, neighbors, mail, and other means), and kind of communication (emotional issues, things, ideas, and other people).

The results of this analysis of variance is displayed in Table 13. These results indicate that the research hypothesis is supported by the data. These are significant main effects in frequency of communication across categories of relationship, method of communication, and kind of communication. Two factors must be taken into account in the interpretation of these results: (1) the analysis was conducted on the entire sample of persons named in all subject's social networks, yielding an analytic sample of 216 and (2) only two persons were specified as belonging to the categories of neighbor and co-worker. This last finding was unexpected and may indicate a response bias in the data collection instrument or a lack of communication between research subjects and their respective neighbors and co-workers.

Table 13
[1]
Analysis of Variance of Communication Patterns
Frequency, Relationship, Method, and Kind

By:
Frequency	Frequency of Emotional Communication
Relationship	Relationship to Subject
Method	Method of Communication
Kind	Kind of Communication

Source of Variation	Sum of Squares	Degrees of Freedom	Mean Square	F Ratio	Level of Significance
MAIN EFFECTS					
Relationship	531.67	5	106.33	28.62	0.0
Method	242.02	3	80.67	18.63	0.0
Kind	84.54	3	28.18	5.68	0.001
Residual		216			

[1]
Total sample. Includes all persons cited in networks of subjects (N=16).

Inspection of the analyses of variance results indicates that frequency of emotional communication with spouse is significantly greater than frequency of emotional communication with any of the other relationship groups. Frequency of emotional communication is also greater for family compared to friends or relatives, and for friends compared to relatives.

Analysis of method of communication indicates that there is significantly more emotional communication in the face to face mode than by telephone, mail or other (non-verbal) means. Also, more emotional communication is reported by telephone than by main. In terms of the frequency and kind of communication the date shows that emotional issues are communicated about more frequently than ideas, things, or other people. In descending order of frequency, the content categories of communications are emotions, other people, things, and ideas. There is no significant difference in the frequency of communication between content categories of emotions and other people.

In conclusion, these results generally support the research hypothesis. However, these results also indicate that arrangement of relationship, method, and kind of communication in descending orders of intimacy are slightly different than expected. This result must be viewed with caution noting that there was an absence of sufficient data in specific categories or relationship to generalize from this sample.

Synopsis of Findings

A synopsis of the salient findings reported here serves to focus the ensuing discussion of these research results. The only empirically significant relationship between social network indicators and affects associated with marital interaction have been found to be the covariation of network indicators and total anxiety. These relationships are different for husbands and wives. Pooling off networks, i.e., combining husband and wife network indicators, does not reveal significant associations.

Table 14 shows the variation in the standardized partial regression coefficients summarized for husbands and wives. The salient point is the relationship of amount of emotional communication (FREQ) to variation in total anxiety. Increased emotional communication

ithin husbands' social network is inversely correlated
ith the level of anxiety; increased emotional
ommunication is directly correlated with level of
nxiety for wives. The magnitude and relative size of
he contribution of network indicators to the entire
egression equations is such that a marital role effect
isappears when the data are pooled. The data, there-
ore, suggest that the process which relates social
etwork to marital interaction is different for
usbands as compared to wives.

Table 14

Summary of Regression Results
for Husbands and Wives (Anxiety)

ariable	H	W
NTRA2	2.52	1.67
NTRA3	1.27	1.35
IZE	.402	.817
NTER	.588	.595
REQ	-2.53	.366

CHAPTER 5

DISCUSSION AND CONCLUSIONS

Briefly, the findings of this study indicate that certain features of social networks are significantly associated with affects found during spousal interaction. The predicted relationships of inverse association of network characteristics with variation in anxiety, total hostility outward, and total hostility inward and ambivalent were not supported by the data. The data show this statement of relationships is not adequate to capture the complexity of a person's interaction with members of their social network. It appears that additional information is needed to fully understand the relationship between social networks and marital interaction. The second research hypothesis concerning the relationship of social network structure and function is supported by the findings reported above. The following discussion seeks to reconcile these findings with current sociological perspectives and delineate the implications of these findings for further research and clinical practice.

Discussion

The data presented appears to be inconsistent with most prevailing assumptions about the function of social networks. The data indicate that structural configurations of social networks are differentially associated with specific emotional outcome of marital interaction. More to the point, the network structure which is associated with anxiety is different from the network structure which is associated with hostility outward, or hostility inward and ambivalent. This

52

finding implies that intervention in social networks must be considered within the context of the desired affective result. Manipulation of a social network to attenuate feelings of anxiety may or may not, at the same time, increase the amount of hostility experienced by the subject.

This finding presents a very complex picture. A person's experience of emotions is not only affected by their social networks, but by the structure of their spouses' network and the interaction of both networks. This conclusion is consistent with the hypothesis proposed by Bott (1957). However, the data indicate that the empirical reality of spousal interaction patterns is far more complex than this linear combination of direct variable effects would predict. The logic of the relationship between network structure and anxiety is not the same as the logic of the relationship between network structure and hostility. The difference may be explained by an examination of an interactional theory of emotions.

Kemper (1978) proposes a theory of emotions which is consistent with the findings of this study. Kemper (1978) first assume that emotions are a by-product of interaction between people. Further, emotions may be categorized as structural, anticipatory, and consequent, dependent upon the time orientation of the person experiencing the emotions. An anticipatory emotion would be one which comes about through a process of visualizing social interaction which may occur in the future. Consequent emotions are those which are a result of actual interaction. Within this context, the dependent variables in the analysis reported here are seen as consequent emotions brought about by interaction with spouse.

Kemper's (1978:47) theory of emotions is extremely complex, containing approximately 1700 separate emotional state possibilities. This social interactional theory of emotions may be briefly summarized as follows: emotions are brought about through a process of social interaction. Specific emotional states are correlated with differentials in power and status relations among social actors. Deficiencies and/or excesses of power and/or status give rise to specific emotional states. Determination of an emotional outcome of social interaction is also dependent upon agency and orientation to other. Agency refers to perceived source of status or power differential. In other words, is self or other seen as the cause of felt deficiencies or excesses of social power and status? Orientation to other is an emotional modifier which either exacerbates or attenuates a basic emotional state. Orientation may be defined along like-dislike continuum. Therefore, in order to determine which emotion will result from a specific interaction, as assessment must be made of the perceived power differential, status differential, subject's attribution of agency, and subject's orientation to other.

A detailed examination of Kemper's (1978) interactional approach to emotions produces the following predictions:

(1) Anxiety results when person perceives a threatened loss of power or status. This state is attenuated with a liking orientation to others.

(2) Interactional status deficiencies result in hostility, inwardly directed when self is seen as agent of deficiency; hostility, outwardly directed when other is seen as agent of deficiency.

(3) Interactional power deficiency results in hostility, outwardly directed when other is perceived as agent.

(4) Interactional power deficiency results in anxiety when self is perceived as agent.

Within this study context, Kemper's (1978) theory predicts, the presence of anxiety and hostility during marital interaction when one spouse perceives the other to be disengaging from the relationship (threat), and when other is seen as agent, hostility outward. In addition, where self was seen as agent, hostility inward would be experienced. Complexity arises when it is realized that all these processes occur simultaneously and ineract with one another.

Interaction with one's own network members may reduce anxiety by reducing social uncertainty and threat of loss; however, interaction with a dislike spouses network would increase anxiety. This pattern is revealed in the data. Interaction with a person's own network members, in an emotional mode, increase self esteem making it more likely that a perceived status or power deficiency is seen as due to other; thus, producing hostility outward. Again this pattern is revealed in the data. Emotionally based interaction with a smaller number of network members is expected to result in reception of less information which attributes agency to other. The less information received indicating other, as agent, leads to increased probability of self being seen as agent and the production of hostility inward and ambivalent. Therefore, the results of the data analysis reported above are consistent with a theoretical explanation offered by Kemper (1978) which attributes emotional states to be the result of social interaction.

Further support for this interpretation of the data may be found in the recent literature regarding theoretical aspects of social networks. Van Pouke (1980) in a paper detailing the network constraints on social action, notes that the type of social control and exchange pattern found in a social network varies according to whether the network is sentiment, interest, or power based. Van Pouke (1980:187) states that power based networks are formed to facilitate the accomplishment of long term goals, such as child nurturance or life long companionship. The social control exerted in a power based network is more constraining to individual behavior than control exerted in other types of networks. The power based network is expected to be closely related to variation in anxiety and hostility affects.

Safilios-Rothschild (1976) states that power distribution among marital partners is a central feature of marital interaction. In her analysis of the structure and dynamics of the marital relationship, Safilios-Rothschild gives preeminence to perceptions of power relationships between husband and wife. Determination of relative power positions among marital partners becomes the most salient feature of spousal interaction and is related to spouses' perception of the nature of their relationship. Therefore, power relationship negotiations are a central, salient feature of marital interactions which is associated with affective states of spouses.

Interpretation of the results of this investigation is complex and includes elements of Kemper's (1978) theory of emotions, network theory, e.g., Bott (1957) and Weiss' (1969) perspectives of the relationship of network structure to function. Kemper (1978) offers an explanation of the process which generated anxiety as a result of social interaction. Giver this study sample it may be concluded that anxiety is generated when one spouse perceived a loss of power in the marital relationship. This perceived power loss is exacerbated when spouse commitment to the relationship is low. In addition, when self is perceived as the agent of power deficiency, anxiety is amplified. Therefore, Kemper (1978) offers a theoretical explanation of the generation of anxiety found in the data analyzed.

Bott's (1957) analysis of social networks and marital role performance was conducted without benefit of explanation of the relationship between social structure and emotions such as given by Kemper (1978). The findings presented here present a further specification of the process which links network structures to affects. The most striking finding in this study is the difference in the covariation of network structure and affect between husbands and wives. This difference may be interpreted to suggest that the network of husbands and wives operate differently in their relationship to the management of affects or emotions. One possible explanation, and the one proposed here, is that the networks of husbands function to provide them with information, in the form of social support, which indicates that other is the agent of the perceived power deficiency. Thus, increased interaction with their social network, in the form of social support, is inversely related to variation in anxiety associated with marital interaction.

Explanation of the difference in this pattern for wives is more problematic. In terms of Kemper's (1978) theory, it appears that wives receive information from their networks that indicates that the agency of a perceived power deficiency is self. When self is perceived as agent, anxiety increases. The data indicate that increased emotional communication within the wives network is associated with an increase in anxiety levels; thus, this interaction leads to an attribution, on the part of wives, of self as agent of the power deficit. Attribution theory, as posited by kelley (1967) may offer an explanation of the rationale behind this apparent "blaming of self". Wheaton (1980), in a discussion of attribution theory as it relates to the sociogenesis of psychological disorder, states that socialization into low status positions, i.e., female versus male child, correlated with low perception of personal power that may carry over into adult role relationships. Therefore, it is expected that wives are more prone to interpret the source of power deficiencies as self. While this rationale remains largely untested, the results reported here indicate that investigation of this phenomenon, in the future, should include indicators of power differentials and perception of agency. In addition, recent research has indicated that the pattern of relationships reported here has been found in other samples of wives. Brown, et.al. (1977), in a study of 154 women in England, found that increased social integration was directly correlated with increased anxiety and inversely correlated with depressive symptomology.

Examination of the data (Table 14) also indicates that specific characteristics of networks, such as size, tend to amplify anxiety. This is an indication that size of network is related to the transmission of a message to the person that they are the agent of a power deficiency. Alternately, the absolute size of a social network may be perceived as a structural mechanism which reduces the absolute social power of a person; and, thus, the network itself, generates anxiety which is manifested in the marital relationship. Further specification of these interaction processes must await further research as the data available for this investigation does not include adequate measures of social status and power differentials among social networks members.

Weiss' (1969) general formulation of social network structure and the functions each segment of networks serves for the individual bear upon the relationships discussed above. Current findings of this study indicate that hypotheses formed upon Weiss's (1969) perspective are supported. Specifically, it was found that a social network may be operationalized in terms of relationship structure, and that these relationships may be arranged along a continuum of decreasing levels of intimacy, when intimacy is defined as emotional communication. That is, spouse, family, friends, and relatives respectively provide decreasing degrees of social support. Therefore, if interaction with spouse is associated with anxiety, the most effective countervailing force would be interaction with family, friends, and then relatives. The association of network structure, either as amplifying or attentuating influence, with affects may be viewed in an ordinal manner. This finding suggests that the theoretical formulations of Weiss (1969) are correct;

57

indentifiable segments of social networks perform specific functions. The segments, operationalized here as relationship categories, provide varying degrees of social support and this support function is associated with a variance in affects.

Studies conducted by Bell and Boat (1957), Brim (1974), Hirsch (1980), and Turkat (1980) provide supporting evidence for this interpretation of the data analyzed in this study. Bell and Boat (1957) report that kinship relations are more likely to be personal, close, and intimate than relationships with friends, neighbors, and co-workers. This relationship appears to hold across different categories of socioeconomic class examined in the urban San Francisco area (Bell and Boat, 1957:391). Brim (1974), in a study of 153 Seattle area women, found that presence of a marital partner was positively correlated with social support derived from the women's networks. Thus, spouse was found to be a conditional factor in the relationship between social networks and positive psychological states. Hirsch (1980) reports that the existence of low density, multidimensional social networks is positively associated with lessened pathological symptomology. Weiss' (1969) perspective and the results reported here are supported by Hirsch's (1980) findings. In a similar vein, Turkat (1980) states that a social network containing diverse sets of role relations has been found to be positively related to improved mental health by clinicians. In brief, there exists ample evidence in the literature that the findings reported here present an accurate picture of the relationship of social network structure to function and the consequent effect social networks have on psychological functioning of the individual.

An explanation of the difference between husbands and wives, in terms of the association of network characteristics with affects, is limited by the data available. This difference could possibly be explained through the immediate effect of a constellation of sociopsychological or biosocial variables. in summary, a difference in the relationship of network characteristics with affects associated with marital interaction has been empirically demonstrated. These defferences are explained by using an interactional theory of emotions, the findings reported in the social network literature, and a structural-functionalist approach to operationalizing social networks. Further investigation of the relationship between social

etworks and marital interaction must include data
hich measures attitudinal and biological
haracteristics of persons in the networks of both
pouses.
A subsidiary finding of this research is the
ecessity of using multiple indicators of network
ensity to demonstrate a relationship between networks
nd affects. The discussion of these indicators in
hapter IV explained the calculus of network density.
hese indicators (INTRA 1, 2, 3) roughly parallel the
ypologies of social networks developed by Laumann
1973): INTRA 1 is an inverse indicator of network
radialty"; INTRA 2 indicates degree of "interlocking"
cross diverse role sets; and INTRA 3 measures non-
ymetrical interactions or extent of role
ifferentiation. Consideration of all three factors is
equired to understand the complexity of network
ffect. The implication of this finding is that
ultiple indicators of network density should be used
n future research involving social networks.

Conclusions

The original research question concerning the
elationship has been found to be far more complex than
he original hypotheses assumed. Networks have been
hown to be associated in different fashions with
istinct affects. These overall relationships also
ary with gender and subject. Role diversity and
onnection between role sets also appears to be a
ritical variable in the association of networks and
sychic states.
The use of Kemper's (1978) theory indicates
ertain factors, not included in the original research
ypotheses have an effect on the relationship of
etwork characteristics to affects. Attribution of
gency and salience of individual network linkages act
s conditional modifiers in the relationship of
etworks and affects. The data provide evidence that a
ocial interactional approach to social networks is a
ruitful analytical perspective. However, additional
ata is required to fully investigate these
elationships.
Two caveats apply to these research results. The
ata does not permit distinguishing this study sample
rom an otherwise comparable non-help seeking group.
s stated earlier, people who seek mental health care

59

tacitly admit the failure of their naturally occurring social networks to provide support. One possibilty explanation for the differences observed between men and women could be related to failures of husbands and wives respective networks to provide adequate support. Further investigation of this issue requires longitudinal study with help seeking and non-help seeking populations. The uniquness of this study sample, i.e., extreme demographic homogeneity and small size, has enhanced the descriptive nature of the results. However, these same factors also limit the generalizability of results. The major benefit realized, within these caveats, is the availability to specify directions for future research which addresses the previously underestimated complexity of social networks.

The implications of this analysis is that future research relating social network characteristics to marital interaction must include detailed measures of the social psychological nature of all individual network linkages. Measurement of interpersonal attraction, salience of relationships, and dimensions of social power and status dimensions are needed. Further, the measurement of specific affective states, such as anxiety and hostility, is required. A major reason why the findings reported here have not been reported previously is that use of complex indicator systems of affects have not been applied to this research problem.

The complexity of the issue, which has not been directly addressed in previous research, is evidenced by the findings reported. These multiple indicators of network density should be included in any future analysis. Based on the results presented here, it is felt that a sociological approach to the study of emotions will yield a better understanding of the effects social structure has upon the individual.

This study was generated by a question posed within the clinical field of psychiatry. The results reported here have implications for clinical practice which have not been explicated in the literature. The pioneering work of Pattison (1975) and Mueller (1980) indicates the importance of the gross relationship of social networks and affective disorders. However, this literature has not specified the nature of these relationships. For example, it has been found in this study that the relationship of network characteristics to affects is different when affects are specified as anxiety or hostility. It also appears that affects themselves are associated with one another. This implies that psychiatric intervention for the management of anxiety may have an opposite effect on the management of hostility, dependent upon the gender of the patient. Therefore, the findings of this study should be taken into account by clinicians who perform active social network interventions. This study implies that the nature of the clinical intervention should vary according to the affective disorder and marital role of the patient.

Finally, the theoretical nature of the relationship among the density measures employed in this study needs to be explored in future work. While it appears that these relationships are somehow connected to the within and across role set ideas of Laumann(1973) and others, no specific exposition of these relationships exists in the literature. The data examined here, although a preliminary reconnaissance, does indicate that these differential role set functions have important implications for clinical practice. In Kemper's parlance, messages of power and status differentials given to a person during communication with other, may be linked directly to the generation of hostility and anxiety. Our data indicate that this broad theoretical formulation may be taken one step farther. It not only matters that power and status differentials are subjectively apparent to the social actor; but it is just as critical to our understanding of this process to know the role set locus of these messages and the nature of the relationship and communication patterns within these discrete role sets. A person's social network is an amalgam of relationships he/she has with people functioning in the capacity of a symbolic role relationship. The extent, strength, persistence and valence of these various symbolic communication links must be explored to arrive at an understanding of the process, external to the individual, which brings about emotional responses.

APPENDIX A

Personal Sphere Model of Social Support Systems

Part I: Drawing

On the third page of this Appendix, draw aroun
the symbol of self, in any way you please, all th
people who have been important in your life. If ther
have been ideas or things of particular importance
include them. Indicate the personal importance of eac
(1) person, (2) idea, or (3) thing by drawing from on
to three lines between yourself and each of these thre
-- one line for those of some importance, two for thos
of moderate importance, and three for those of grea
importance.

If a relationship has been interrupted, indicat
this fact by crossing these connecting lines with on
to three crossbars for the most severe interruption
two for those of moderate, and one for those of lesse
interruption. Indicate deceased with the letter D.

Four different examples of drawings are shown o
the second page of this Appendix. Feel free t
innovate and make your own drawing as different as yo
wish.

62

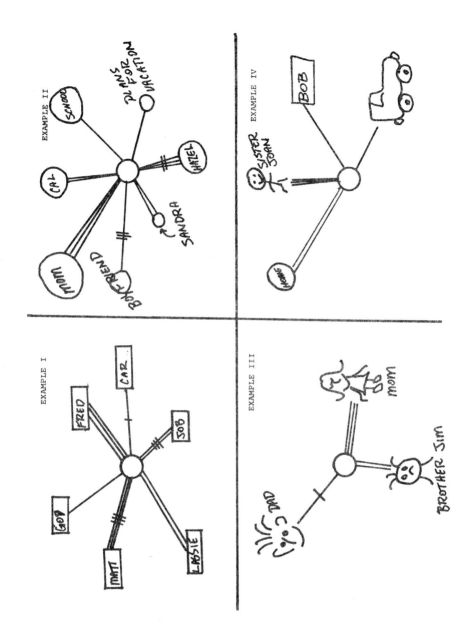

EXAMPLE I

EXAMPLE II

EXAMPLE III

EXAMPLE IV

63

Instructions: (read before beginning)

Part II: Drawing-Identification

Now, identify all items in your drawing on the attached identification table, page 6. Use only first names to designate people to insure confidentiality of your responses. To clarify the categories in the table noted the examples below:

People - spouse (sp), immediate family members (fa), (e.g., parents, children), relatives (r), friends (fr), neighbors (n), and co-workers (co). Things - objects either physical (e.g., car, house, etc.), living (e.g., pets or animals), or deceased, label with capital (D). Other - ideas, etc.

1. Write down first names for all the people you have drawn in column 1 (People-Relationship). Next to their name in column 1 place the lower case symbol (sp, fa, r, fr, n, co) which identifies this person's relationship to you.

2. Next to each person, write in column 2 the number which corresponds to how frequently you communicate with each other, according to the following scale:

```
0 = less than once a year
1 = about once a year
2 = about once a month
3 = once every week
4 = twice a week
5 = every two or three days
6 = once a day
7 = more than once a day
```

3. Column 3 refers to how you communicate. Enter the appropriate code letter(s) in column 3 which refers to the person: p = telephone, m = mail, f = face to face conversation, and o = any other interaction such as non-verbal communication. You may enters as many letters as apply.

4. Column 4 refers to the kinds of communication you usually have with each person on your drawing. Use the following code to indicate the kinds of

65

<u>communication</u> you have with these people.

> E = communication about feelings and <u>emotions</u> such as sadness or joy
> I = communicating about <u>ideas</u> or concepts such as politics or unemployment
> T = communicating about physical objects such as cars, houses or the weather (i.e., <u>things</u>)
> P = communicating about <u>people</u> other than yourself

For example, if you talked to a neighbor about "physical objects", you would place a "T" in column 4 on the line with the neighbor's first name. If you talk to one person about several kinds of things, list them in the order of the most common topic first, e.g., E, I, T. For example, an entry in column 4 such as "E, I, T" would mean that you talked to that person about Emotions most, Ideas a little less and Things least of all.

5. Column 5 refers to <u>who communicates with whom</u> in your list of people. Notice that there are numbers next to each person named in column 1. Use these numbers to indicate which of the people talk to other people listed in column 1. The purpose is to determine from the list which people are important to you: who knows and communicates with whom on the list. For example, if the person named on the first line in column 1 (person #1) communicates at least once a month with the person named on lines #3 and #5, you would place number 3 and 5 in column 5, line 1. Note the example in the table. It indicates person #1 communicates with persons #3 and #5.

Identification of People, Ideas, and Things in Personal Sphere Drawing

	Column 1	Column 2	Column 3	Column 4	Column 5	Column 6
	People-Relationship	Frequency	How	Kind	Connections	(leave blank)
EXAMPLE	Ralph fa	2	P	I,W,T	3, 5	
(1)						
(2)						
(3)						
(4)						
(5)						
(6)						
(7)						
(8)						
(9)						
(10)						
(11)						
(12)						

APPENDIX B

This appendix contains supplementary data analysis
tables.   This data reports the non-significant results
of   the analysis and is intended to provide   additional
information to the interested reader.

TABLE A

HUSBAND NETWORK INDICATORS

Dependent Variable: HC7P (Anxiety)

Independent Variable in Regression	Beta	P	R2
First Order Regressions Non-Significant			
Two Variable Regressions Non-Significant			
Three Variable Regressions Non-Significant			
Four Variable Regressions			
INTRA 1	2.553	.097	.879
INTRA 3	1.576		
FREQ	-2.924		
INTER	0.544		
INTRA 2	2.018	.017	.963
INTRA 3	1.011		
FREQ	-2.309		
INTER	0.579		
Five Variable Regressions			
INTRA 1	2.247	.014	.994
INTRA 3	1.343		
FREQ	-2.947		
SIZE	-0.518		
INTER	0.594		
INTRA 2	2.526	.016	.993
INTRA 3	1.277		
FREQ	-2.537		
SIZE	0.402		
INTER	0.588		

69

TABLE B

WIFE NETWORK INDICATORS

Dependent Variable: WC7P (Anxiety)
Independent Variable

in Regression	Beta	P	R2
INTER	.592	.121	.350
INTRA 1	1.340	.165	.512
INTRA 3	1.130		
INTRA 1	.378	.182	.493
INTER	.588		
INTRA 1	1.324	.039	.850
INTRA 3	1.118		
INTER	.582		
INTRA 1	1.606	.100	.757
INTRA 3	1.328		
SIZE	.515		
INTRA 2	1.804	.057	.819
INTRA 3	1.294		
SIZE	1.102		
INTRA 1	1.402	.026	.950
INTRA 3	1.359		
FREQ	.430		
INTER	.811		
INTRA 1	1.485	.054	.919
INTRA 3	1.238		
SIZE	.305		
INTER	.450		
INTRA 2	1.636	n.s.	
INTRA 3	1.182		
SIZE	.865		
INTER	.375		
INTRA 1	1.521	.018	.992
INTRA 3	1.424		
FREQ	.376		
SIZE	.244		
INTER	.677		

70

TABLE B

WIFE NETWORK INDICATORS

Dependent Variable: WC7P (Anxiety)

Independent Variable

in Regression	Beta	P	R2
INTRA 2	1.670	.005	.997
INTRA 3	1.358		
FREQ	.366		
SIZE	.817		
INTER	.595		

TABLE C

HUSBAND NETWORK INDICATORS

Dependent Variable:

H13P (Hostility,   Inward and Ambivalent)

Independent Variable

in Regression	Beta	P	R2
INTRA 2	.624	.098	.389
FREQ	.653	.078	.427
INTRA 2	.271	.222	.451
FREQ	.432		
INTRA 2	.216	.368	.509
FREQ	.421		
INTRA	-.249		
INTRA 2	.427	.584	.525
INTRA 3	.192		
FREQ	.188		
INTER	-.204		

71

BIBLIOGRAPHY

Aldous, Joan
    1977 "Family Interaction Patterns." Annual Review
        of Sociology 3: 105-135, Annual Reviews, Inc.

Aldous, Joan and Strauss, M. A.
    1966 "Social Networks and Conjugal Roles: A Test
        of Bott's Hypothesis." Social Forces 44:
        576-580.

Barnes, J. A.
    1954 "Class and Committees in the Norwegian Island
        Parish." Human Relations 7 (1).

Bateson, Gregory
    1979 Mind and Nature. New York: Dutton.

Bell, W and Boat, M. D.
    1957 "Urban Neighborhoods and Informal Social
        Relations." American Journal of Sociology,
        62; 391-398.

Blood, R. O.
    1969 "Kinship and Interaction and Marital
        Solidaritry." Merrill Palmer Quarterly 15:
        171-184.

Boissevain, J.
    1974 Friends of Friends: Networks, Manipulators
        and Coalitions. New York: St. Martin's
        Press.

Bott, E.
    1957 Family and Social Network. London:
        Tavistock.

72

Brim, J. A.
  1974 "Social Network Correlates of Avowed
       Happiness," The Journal of Nervous and
       Mental Disease, 158: 432-439.

Brown, G. W,, Davidson, S., Harris, T., Maclean, U.,
       Pollock, S., and Prudo, R.
  1977 "Psychiatric Disorder in London and North
       Uist," Social Science and Medicine, 11:
       367-377.

Brown, E. P. (Ed.)
  1977 Biomedical Computer Program P Series.
       Berkeley: University of California Press.

Buckley, Walter
  1967 Sociology and Modern Systems Theory.
       Englewood Cliffs: Prentice-Hall.

Cassel, J.
  1976 "The Contribution of the Social Environment
       to Host Resistance." The Fourth Wade Hampton
       Frost Lecture, American Journal of
       Epidemiology 1: 347-314.

Dhrymes, P. J.
  1978 Introductory Econometrics. New York:
       Springer-Verlag.

Durkheim, Emile
  1951 Suicide. New York: Free Press.

Fischer, C., Jackson, R. M., Stueve, C. A., Gerson,
       K., Jones, L. M., and Baldassare, M.
  1976 Networks and Places. New York: The Free
       Press.

Frankenberg, R.
  1969 Communities in Britain. London: Penguin.

Gottschalk, L. A. and Glesser, G. C.
  1969 The Measurement of Psychological States
       Through the Content Analysis of Verbal
       Behavior. Los Angeles: University of
       California Press.

Gottschalk, L. A., Winger, C. N., and Glesser, G. C.
  1969 Manual of Instructions for Using the

Gottschalk-Gleser Content Analysis Scales:
Anxiety, Hostility and Social Alienation-
Personal Disorganization. Berkeley:
University of California Press.

Granovetter, M.
1973 "The Strength of Weak Ties." American
Journal of Sociology 78 (May) 9: 1360-1380.

Harrell-Bond, B. E.
1969 "Conjugal Role Behavior". Human Relations
(22): 77-91.

Henderson, S.
1977 "The Social Network, Support and Neurosis."
British Journal of Psychiatry (131): 185-
191.

1980 "A Development in Social Psychiatry: The
Systematic Study of Social Bonds." Journal
of Nervous and Mental Disease, 168 (2): 63-
69.

Hirsch, B. J.
1980 "Natural Support Systems and Coping with
Major Life Changes." American Journal of
Community Psychology, 8: 159-172.

Hyman, Martin D.
1967 "Medicine" in Lazarsfeld, et. al. (ed.). The
Uses of Sociology. New York: Basic.

Jackson, R. M., Fischer, C. S., and Jones, L. M.
1977 "The Dimensions of Social Networks." Pp. 39-
58 in Fischer et. al., Networks and Places.
New York: Free Press.

Kelley, H. H.
1967 "Attribution Theory of Social Psychology."
Pp. 192-237 in D. Levine (Ed.), The Nebraska
Symposium on Motivation, Vol. 15. Lincoln:
University of Nebraska Press.

Kemper, T. D.
1978 "Toward a Sociology of Emotions." American
Sociologist, 13: 30-41.

Kessler, R. C.

1979 "Stress, Social Status, and Psychological Distress." Journal of Health and Social Behavior 20: 259-272.

aumann, E. O.
1973 Bonds of Pluralism. New York: Wiley.

einhardt, S.
1977 Social Networks: A Developing Paradigm. New York: Academic Press.

evine, D. N., Cater, E. B., and Gorman, E. M.
1976 "Simmel's Influence on Americal Sociology." American Journal of Sociology 81 (4): 813-845.

1976 "Simmel's Influence on American Sociology II." American Journal of Sociology 81 (5): 1112-1132.

ewin, K.
1935 A Dynamic Theory of Personality. New York: McGraw-Hill.

eim, R. and Leim, J.
1978 "Social Class and Mental Illness Reconsidered: The Role of Economic Stress and Social Support." Journal of Health and Social Behavior 19: 139-156.

endell, D. and Fischer, S.
1958 "A Multi-generational Approach to Treatment of Psychotherapy." Journal of Nervous and Mental Disease 126: 523-259.

itchell, J. C. (Ed.)
1969 Social Network in Urban Situation. Manchester, England: University of Manchester Press.

euller, Daniel P.
1980 "Social Networks: A Promising Direction for Research on the Relationship of the Social Environment to Psychiatric Disorder." Social Science and Medicine 14A: 134-161.

yers, Jerome K.
1965 "The Study of Mental Illness" in Gouldner and

Miller (eds.) Applied Sociology. New York: Free Press.

Nelson, J. I.
1966 "Clique Contacts and Family Orientations." American Sociological Review 31: 663-672.

Nie, N. N., Hull, C. H., Jenkins, J. G., Steinbrenner, K, and Bent, D. H.
1975 Statistical Package for the Social Sciences (2nd Edition). New York: McGraw-Hill.

Pattison, E. M.
1973 "Social System Psychotherapy." American JHournal of Psychotherapy 18: 396-409.

Pattison, E. M., DeFrancisco, D., Wood, P., Frazier, H., and Crowder, J.
1975 "A Psychosocial Kinship Model for Family Therapy." American Journal of Psychiatry 132 (12): 1246-1251.

Pattison, E. M.
1977 "A Theoretical-Empirical Base for Social System Therapy" in Foulks, Wintrob, Westermeyer and Favazza (eds.) Current Perspectives in Cultural Psychiatry, Spectrum: New York.

Ramey, J. W.
1975 "Intimate Groups and Networks: Frequent Consequences of Sexually Open Marriage." The Family Coordinator, October, (24): 515-530.

Safilios-Rothschild, C.
1976 "The Dimensions of Power Distribution in the Family." in Contemporary Marriage; Structure, Dynamics, and Therapy. (Grunebaum and Christ, eds.) Boston: Little, Brown and Company.

SAS Institute, Inc.
1979 SAS User's Guide: 1979 Edition, Raliegh, North Carolina.

Schmeideck, R. A.
1978 The Personal Sphere Model. New York: Grune and Stratton.

76

Silbergeld, S. R., Manderscheid, R. W. and O'Neill, P. M.
1976 "Free Association Anxiety and Hostility: View from a Junior High School". Psychological Reports 37: 495-504.

Silbergeld, S. R., Manderscheid, R. W.
1976 "Dyadic Free Association." Psychological Reports (39): 423-426.

Simmel, Georg
1902 "The Number of Members as Determining the Sociological Form of the Group," American Journal oif Sociology VIII (1): 1-46.

Simmel, Georg
1902 "Group Expansion and Development of Individuality" in Georg Simmel (1908) on Individuality and Social Forces. D. N. Levine (ed.), pp. 251-293. Chicago: University of Chicago Press.

Slater, P.
1961 "Social Limitations on Libidinal Withdrawal." American Journal of Sociology 67 (3): 269 - 311.

Toomey, D. M.
1971 "Conjugal Roles and Social Networks in an Urban Working Class Sample." Human Relations 24 (5): 417-431.

Turkat, D.
1980 "Social Networks: Theory and Practice," Journal of Commuinity Psychology 8: 99-109.

Turner, C.
1967 "Conjugal Roles and Social Networks: A Re-Examination of a Hyupothesis." Human Relations 20: 121-130.

Udry, J. R. and Hall, M.
1965 "Marital Role Segregation and Social Networks in Middle-Class, Middle-Aged Couples." Journal of Marriage and the Family 27: 392-395.

Van Poucke, W.
    1980 "Network Constraints on Social Action:
        Preliminaries for a Network Theory," Social
        Networks 2: 181-190.

    1976 "Neighborhood and Community Contexts in Help
        Seeking, Problem Coping, and Mental Health."
        Data Analysis Monograph. Program in
        Community Effectiveness, University of
        Michigan.

Weiss, R. S.
    1969 "The Fund of Sociability." Transaction 6
        (9): 36-43.

    1974 "The Provisions of Social Relationships."
        Pp. 17-26 in Z. Rubin (ed.). Doing Unto
        Others. Prentice-Hall.

Wheaton, B.
    1980 "The Sociogenesis of Psychological Disorder:
        An Attributional Theory." Journal of Health
        and Social Behavior 21: 100-124.

Wolff, Kurt H.
    1950 The Sociology of Georg Simmel, New York: The
        Free Press.